THE

FIRST-TIME
MANAGER
HR

T0243803

THE
FIRST-TIME
MANAGER

PAUL FALCONE

HarperCollins
Leadership

An Imprint of HarperCollins

Published by HarperCollins Leadership, an imprint of HarperCollins Focus LLC.

Any internet addresses, phone numbers, or company or product information printed in this book are offered as a resource and are not intended in any way to be or to imply an endorsement by HarperCollins Leadership, nor does HarperCollins Leadership vouch for the existence, content, or services of these sites, phone numbers, companies, or products beyond the life of this book.

ISBN 978-1-4002-4234-4 (eBook)
ISBN 978-1-4002-4233-7 (TP)

Library of Congress Cataloging-in-Publication Data
Library of Congress Cataloging-in-Publication application has been submitted.

Printed in the United States of America
24 25 26 27 28 LBC 5 4 3 2 1

CONTENTS

PART THREE

Strategic HR and the Future of the HR Profession   161

PERMISSIONS

The following materials were taken from articles written by Paul Falcone:

INTRODUCTION

Welcome to the world of human resources *management*. And I mean that in two ways: first, you've likely been part of the world of human resources management for some time now. More significantly, you've graduated to the rank of manager recently and purchased this book to help you master the challenges that are sure to come your way across the full spectrum of the HR discipline—from recruitment and employee relations to compensation and benefits to training and HR information systems (HRIS) and much more. As you're likely aware, HR is a tremendously broad field with new responsibilities and challenges coming our way all the time.

My goal in writing this book for the renowned *First-Time Manager* series will be to take a "coaching approach" with you, the reader, and welcome you to sit side by side with a more seasoned HR executive who can show you the ropes, teach you shortcuts, and help you come up to speed in the many diverse aspects of the HR discipline in your organization. Of course, if you're reading this book in hopes of becoming a manager in HR at some point in the not-too-distant future, you've likewise come to the right place as well. This should help you broaden your understanding of the many business aspects of leadership and talent development within your organization and shorten your learning curve significantly.

First, a bit about me. I was honored to serve as the chief human resources officer (CHRO) of the Nickelodeon Animation Studio in Burbank, California. I was also head of international HR for

Paramount Pictures—both companies fell under the umbrella of Viacom at the time (today's Paramount Global), where I worked for just shy of a decade. In my most recent HR role, I served for five years as the CHRO of the Motion Picture and Television Fund (MPTF)—a health-care nonprofit dedicated to the needs of entertainment industry veterans, primarily in its capacity as a residential care facility for the elderly and a skilled nursing facility that included memory care and behavioral psychiatry. In prior positions, I worked as a managing director of HR in the biotech/bioscience space, and I likewise served as head of employee and labor relations for the City of Hope Cancer Center, a renowned hospital and research facility globally recognized for its achievements in the oncology and diabetes space. Finally, I worked in financial services at a private equity firm where I was responsible for recruiting C-level talent (that is, CEOs, CFOs, and COOs) for the firm's newly acquired portfolio companies. I spent three decades in the frontline trenches of HR across multiple industries and in fairly diverse environments—Fortune 500, nonprofit, union, international, and small to midsized firms—that provided me a breadth of experience into the varying aspects of HR management and leadership.

Aside from my direct work experience, I taught at UCLA Extension's School of Business and Management for well over a decade in their HR professional designation program, highlighting many of the concepts that we're about to address together. I've been a leadership trainer for the American Management Association, a keynote speaker at various HR conferences, and I'm also a long-term columnist for the Society of Human Resource Management's *HR Magazine* and *HR Daily Newsletter*. In 2022, I launched my own consulting firm, Paul Falcone Workplace Leadership Consulting, focusing on (1) management and leadership training, (2) executive coaching, (3) international keynote speaking, and (4) HR advisory services. I recognize and am grateful for the fact that I've gotten opportunities to experience and contribute to some great companies, and I've had some fantastic mentors along the way.

My goal now is to bottle all of these various experiences into one book to help you maximize your career opportunities within the HR space. Specifically, I hope to:

- round out your exposure to the full gamut of disciplines and specialties within the HR suite of services;
- share deeper-dive knowledge and insights into specific areas of the HR world to shortcut the natural learning curve;
- maximize certain features of HR programs and service offerings to help you attract, develop, and retain top talent;
- raise red flags in areas that could potentially expose you or your organization to unwanted legal liability;
- help you master the levers of HR so that you can perform agilely and skillfully across the full HR spectrum—even if you have only limited exposure at this point to all the subdisciplines within the HR space; and
- provide a tool for your own personal and professional development as you progress within your HR career.

We'll approach the material together, as if I'm your coach and mentor, making even complex concepts easy to understand and explain to others, while avoiding typical pitfalls and roadblocks that others have had to learn through hard-won experience. (There's nothing wrong with that, of course, but this book should help you catapult over a number of obstacles that people often miss and that could come back to bite a newer manager who might not have had exposure to some of the underlying challenges inherent in the HR practice.)

Further, my goal is to make you your clients' "favorite HR person," not only because you listen well to their business needs and care about them personally, but also because you rock your area of HR expertise and know your stuff. People respect competence. They're drawn to people who are passionate about what they do. And they often come to HR when they feel vulnerable and in need of someone with exceptional people leadership abilities who can help them out of a jam. This book will provide you with a fuller understanding of many of the tools, resources, and programs at your fingertips to help strengthen the muscle of your organization's frontline operational leadership team, inspire your employees to fall in love with your company, and move your organization forward in a healthy, creative, and compliant way.

It's an honor for me to join you on such a noble path. It's an incredible opportunity for me to give back to the field that gave me a career for three decades and to pay it forward to newer generations of HR professionals as a way of thanking those who mentored me. Know that you're not alone and that we're in this together. The two of us will make our way through some of the complexities in the HR space, the history and laws that have created today's modern workplace, and—yes—even some of the quirky human behaviors that show themselves from time to time when people are feeling vulnerable or frightened. Consider this book a handy guide and a guiding hand to accompany you each step of the way, something that not only explains the salient elements of the various HR disciplines but that helps you gain deeper-dive knowledge and wisdom beyond your years of experience. We'll walk through this together, step-by-step, building on previous lessons and sharing hard-won insights from a more seasoned practitioner in the field who also happens to be a teacher, lecturer, and keynote speaker.

In many ways, we've lost the ability as a society to sit around the campfire, share a peace pipe, and have elders pass wisdom down to the younger generations. Consider this our HR campfire, our safe place to explore the HR discipline together while I have your back. I hope this book leads to multiple aha moments, shares insights that inspire even more curiosity on your part, and provides a foundation for your career that you can rely on and access again at any point in the future. Let's jump right in and begin our journey together—I'm really excited to walk this path with you . . .

Paul Falcone
Los Angeles, 2024

PART ONE

CORE HR LEADERSHIP PRINCIPLES THAT DRIVE YOUR BUSINESS

OPENING ADVICE

I PLAN TO START EACH MAJOR SECTION of this book with some high-level career guidance to help you see the forest and not just the trees. A common problem facing new managers is that many of the things that made them successful individual contributors won't actually help them as people leaders. For example, newly minted HR managers often try and take over for poorer performing staff members instead of training them how to perform at a higher level. They rarely have the time to do that, of course, yet they stretch themselves thin to do so, often to the detriment of the team.

Here's what it often looks like for first-time managers. There's an expression that says, "What got you here won't get you there." In this case, what made you successful as an individual contributor won't necessarily help you as a people leader. There's a shift in mindset that is required that, unfortunately, many managers never make. And it all has to do with control. What you can guarantee as an individual contributor is that you're in control of everything on your desk, everything you submit, and everything that you recommend. Not so with managers: now your "work product" and "deliverables" are contingent upon other members of your team. But they carry your name with them on everything they produce— good or bad.

If you're not successful transitioning from an individual contributor to a manager mindset, you'll focus on controlling everything in your path. And that translates to micromanagement. Micromanagement stems from a paranoia and fear that you're no longer aware of everything being generated from your team. Don't go there. No one wants to work for a micromanager. Developing a reputation for übercontrol won't help you scale your career, and you'll run yourself ragged in the process. In other words, if you get bogged down managing four people, you may never have a chance to get to supervise forty or four hundred.

Of course, you have the right to see final products and recommendations before they leave your office. But train your team in their craft. (This book will surely help!) Set expectations clearly regarding what you'll want to see and when. Give people the room and discretion to find their own solutions and ways of doing things. See yourself as a mentor and coach rather than a unilateral decision-maker or disciplinarian. You won't have all the answers and don't have to: leadership is a team sport based on collaboration. The changing role of leadership in today's schizophrenic and crisis-driven world focuses on authenticity, trust, agility, and emotional intelligence. Be there to support your team. Have their backs. And build their self-confidence. But always hold them to high performance standards while doing so.

You'll be loved rather than feared, sought after rather than avoided, and praised rather than chided when you're not in the room. Simply put, strive to become your people's favorite boss by training them, communicating expectations clearly, and setting high expectations for results. People will shine when they feel they can do their very best work every day with peace of mind while you help them deliver results and master their craft so they can progress in their own careers over time.

1

EMERGING TRENDS, IMMEDIATE DEMOGRAPHIC CHALLENGES, AND THE FUTURE OF WORK

TALENT. TALENT ACQUISITION. Talent management. Talent development. Whatever way you look at it, *talent* remains the defining asset that drives a company's business and the primary profit lever that differentiates superstar organizations from those that struggle. It's always been that way. Today, however, the value of talent is more recognized and appreciated than ever. The COVID pandemic helped shine a light on how critical it is to have the right talent in place to keep your doors open and your cash flowing. But that was only a beginning, a sliver of light that pointed toward a whole new twenty-first-century paradigm. In fact, one of the key defining variables of organizational success for the remainder of this century will lie in talent acquisition and development. Let's look at why from a historical perspective.

GENERATIONAL NAMES AND IDENTITIES

First, here's how today's working generations of "talent" line up, as a point of reference:

	GENERATION	BORN	SIZE
1	The Traditionalist (a.k.a. "Silent") Generation	1928–45	55 million
2	The Baby Boomer Generation	1946–64	75 million
3	Generation X (a.k.a. "The Baby Bust" Generation)	1965–80	44 million
4	Generation Y (Millennials)	1981–96	80 million
5	Generation Z (Zoomers)	1997–2012	68 million

Note that, as of this writing, millennials and Gen Z comprise approximately 38 percent of the US workforce, and that percentage is increasing exponentially as the baby boomers move toward full retirement around 2029.

In fairness, the workplace has never been a single-generation monopoly. Junior workers have always focused on gaining experience and advancing their careers. Senior workers have always served as supervisors and mentors. And there's always been some tension between the two. That's to be expected. But workplaces generally employed Americans from two or (at most) three generations, not five. As one might expect, this phenomenon affects the workforce in both subtle and overt ways, especially when compounded by rapid changes in technology and communication tools. It's not uncommon to see seventy-seven-year-olds and recent high school graduates on the same teams and in the same departments. That's a consideration we'll explore further in the book.

MILLENNIAL AND GEN Z PRIORITIES

Gen-Y millennials and Gen-Z Zoomers are the most studied generational cohorts in world history. Employers know their priorities and would be wise to direct their workforce planning and cultural enrichment efforts to accommodating their desires and goals, which include:

- career and professional development;
- diversity of thoughts, ideas, and voices;
- an ethical employer, meaningful work, and a management team that cares about them personally;
- work-life-family balance, control, and equilibrium; and
- corporate social responsibility and environmentalism.

These top five desires will remain our priority throughout the book as well because they're clearly defined and relatively easy to build our strategies around. Granted, we're not attempting to place people in boxes by their birth year; but generational norms are shifting. For example, junior employees want positive reinforcement frequently (Gen Y and Gen Z). There is a desire for more flexibility among people who are advanced in their careers and have family commitments (Gen X and baby boomers). Generations are clues, not boxes, but we would be wise to track and trend what's most important to our workers depending on their age and stage of life (which, of course, includes the generation they belong to).

DEMOGRAPHIC SHIFTS

The baby boom began after World War II in 1946 and ended in 1964 with the introduction of the birth control pill. Seventy-five million babies were born over that eighteen-year period—some ten thousand per day. What occurred in 2011 garnered few headlines but was critical to America's future labor supply: the first baby boomers turned sixty-five, and from 2011 to 2029, ten thousand Americans per day retire. Combine this with the fact that the baby boom was followed by the "baby bust" (a.k.a. Gen X), a generation only roughly half its size, and you've got a formula for massive labor shortfalls. True, the Gen-Y millennials are actually bigger than the baby boomers with eighty million constituents, but there will be a lag before they can fully replace aging boomers.

FALLING LABOR FORCE PARTICIPATION RATES

COVID shone a light on talent scarcity, but a declining labor force participation rate adds significantly to the mix and will extend far beyond the pandemic postintegration phase. The labor force participation rate fell from 67 percent in 2000 to roughly 60 percent as of this writing and is projected to remain at that lower level through 2050.

DECLINING GLOBAL BIRTH RATES IN
INDUSTRIALIZED NATIONS

By 2050, advanced industrial countries will be losing population at a dramatic rate, making this a global phenomenon. While the world population hit eight billion for the first time in 2022, the majority of those births took place in underdeveloped, agricultural societies where newborns are needed to ensure the security of aging parents (that is, in nations where there are few social safety nets like Social Security to provide income for basic living needs). As George Friedman pointed out in his *New York Times* bestseller, *The Next Hundred Years*, "living with underpopulation" will remain the norm for the remainder of this century. By the 2040s, many industrialized nations will be enticing tax-paying foreign workers to enter their borders. Some, like Japan and South Korea, have already begun offering foreign workers financial incentives and fast tracks to citizenship.

A NEW TALENT POOL

Today, underrepresented ethnic groups account for 30 percent of the total US population. By 2060, they are expected to reach 60 percent of the population. These groups have historically been overlooked but have a growing amount of buying power. As such, a diverse talent pool increases the range of human capital available to American companies while also better reflecting the buying habits of a more diverse consumer base. This is likely the most critical benefit of diversity hiring: it represents a concrete and reasonable way to develop external talent pools going forward.

This is likewise a core business driver of the DEI&B movement: Diversity, equity, inclusion, and belonging are not only the right things to do for the sake of ethics, morality, and equality of opportunity. DEI&B likewise serves a fundamental business need of supplying untapped talent to fill critical future employment openings. Simply put, organizations that prioritize DEI&B tend to attract a wider range of candidates from different backgrounds and with different experiences. This, in turn, can help companies tap into talent pools that they might otherwise have missed.

We can expect to see a growing focus on "talent development" and "talent management" as a result. External "talent acquisition" will remain in high demand, of course, but wise organizations will look to "grow their own" by focusing their energies and dollars on developing talent rather than simply assuming that posting a job ad or even calling a headhunter will guarantee them superior results. There's no doubt about it: tapping into underrepresented and diverse talent pools will likely be America's lifeline moving forward into the twenty-first century. Wise employers will seize that opportunity by getting ahead of the game and developing a talent bench that reflects their customer base.

Finally, we can expect the future of work to revolve around technological advances that will exceed any of our current expectations. Artificial intelligence, quantum computing, cognitive technology, machine learning, and robotic-process automation (RPA) represent some of the most advanced tools available to measure human capital talent as a true corporate asset. As you move forward in your career, you can expect generative artificial intelligence (AI) to unify data, build rich profiles, minimize unconscious or implicit bias, and build cognitive aptitudes that allow for conversations with employees and job applicants. AI will likewise select appropriate training recommendations that feed individuals' career and professional development needs that dwarf today's capabilities. Data metrics and analytics will drive future strategic recommendations and decision-making, undergirding our talent planning efforts.

It goes without saying: human resources as a discipline within corporate America has a tremendous future due to the scarcity of qualified talent that will be available over the coming decades. As an HR practitioner and manager, you'll likewise have the opportunity to train frontline operational leaders and build management muscle that will help those leaders communicate more effectively, build stronger teams, and positively influence your organization's culture. Combined with the technological tools that are now or will soon be at your disposal, you'll be able to influence your organization's primary profit lever—its talent—and measure and manage increases in performance and productivity that will create a significant return on investment (ROI). Now *that's* something to be excited about!

THE OPPORTUNITIES AND CHALLENGES IN HR'S FUTURE

The opportunities that we just discussed are impressive. It's an exciting time to join the ranks of human resource management because of the tremendous potential that the future holds. With constant change comes multiple opportunities. But you may sometimes feel like the "Be careful what you wish for" maxim applies here. As a human resources manager, you'll face a variety of challenges in today's fast-paced and rapidly changing business environment as well. Let's look at just some of the ways these challenges and opportunities might manifest themselves in your world.

- The Great Resignation, the Gray Resignation, the Great Regret, quiet quitting, quiet firing, and so many other epithets have developed in recent years for good reason: the economy lurches back and forth between talent scarcity and layoffs. The schizophrenic pressures and "poly-crises" of global wars, corporate slowdowns, introductions of new technology, stock market and interest rate gyrations, political turmoil, gun violence, climate change, and so many other critical factors to our society today constantly pervade the workplace. Simply put, many employees are exhausted, confused, and overwhelmed. The pace of change will likewise only exacerbate the situation, leaving workers constantly putting out fires, both at work and at home. Where do we as HR professionals step in to help? Do we draw a line between employees' personal experiences and work demands when both are so closely tied together?

- Gen-Z Zoomers are the youngest cohort in the workplace as of this writing. (Gen Alpha follows next for those born between 2010 and 2024.) We know that Zoomers identify as the loneliest and most isolated generation on the planet due to the social limitations of digital technology. Reports of depression, anxiety, and even suicidal considerations run high among this group, necessitating the need for mental-health and mindfulness benefits. What is HR's role and what can we do to support the members of this generation and the future of our workforce?

- Remote work is likely here to stay. Necessitated by the COVID pandemic and empowered by the introduction of videoconferencing technology like Zoom and Microsoft Teams, we're learning how to make "remote work" work. But balancing autonomy and accountability remains a challenge, especially since they don't teach remote leadership in business schools or corporate classrooms for the most part. We're building the plane while flying it. Balancing employees' needs for work-life-family control and equilibrium with CEOs' "productivity paranoia" about getting work done, managing the unseen, or fostering collaboration hang in the balance. And how do we return people to the office or shop floor on a more regular basis without triggering mass resignations or employee hostility?

- Compliance relative to the many laws and regulations governing the workplace will remain at the top of your priority list, especially if you operate in multiple states. Just to keep things in perspective, many disciplines within corporate America remain challenged by regulatory compliance. But employment laws change quickly, depending on who's in political office and what they deem worth fighting for. No doubt about it—you'll need roller skates to keep up with the many legal and legislative changes coming your way. Most important, know when to escalate matters to your boss, in-house legal counsel, or qualified external employment counsel so that you can get any "hot potatoes" off your lap and share potential liability with those appointed to make such decisions.

- Benefit costs are skyrocketing to accommodate the needs of older Americans, and those increased prices are being passed along to your workforce. Balancing competitive benefits with your budget will remain a significant challenge, and you have only so many cost levers to exercise when you plan for next year's open enrollment: plan design optimization and steerage, contribution strategy, eligibility management, leveraging narrow or custom networks, and pharmacy management. What new benefit offerings will help attract and retain talent? Where can you reinvent the salary / benefits / job security trade-off with workers' discretionary effort and willingness to go above and beyond for the organization? And how do you pay competitively, especially in light of recent salary-history bans, geographic differentials associated with remote work, and cost-of-living adjustments that vary by country (if you're in the international HR space)?

- Mergers and acquisitions, private equity stewardship, professional employer organizations (PEOs), the gig economy, international human resources expansion, flatter organizations, career plateaus, and the list goes on . . . You can specialize in various HR disciplines or work with specialty companies (start-ups, for example) as you build your HR brand, but as a first-time HR manager, you'll want to be able to speak fluently about most of these broader trends, challenges, and opportunities and how they affect your chosen field of specialty.

We've got our work cut out for us. Let's delve deeper into the world of human resource management, talent planning, legal compliance, and people strategy. There's so much for us to learn together!

2

STRATEGIC SOURCING,
RECRUITMENT, SELECTION,
AND ONBOARDING

THE COVID-19 PANDEMIC of the early 2020s opened our eyes as employers to what true labor scarcity looked and felt like. Most executives would describe it as scary: organizations kept their doors open in early 2020 through the disabling period of the pandemic, only to find no human beings to do the work once the public returned to the scene to resume purchasing around 2022–23. A new phrase was coined, the *sansdemic*—meaning "without people"—that kept companies on the brink of closure while determining who would do the work to increase revenue after several years of income scarcity. COVID taught many of us that life wasn't a game, this isn't a dress rehearsal, and after watching more than a million Americans lose their lives to the disease, that life is too short to waste precious time in jobs or careers that lacked a greater purpose or otherwise worked us to death.

People opted to leave their positions and not look back. The reasoning went something like this: "I don't know what I'm going to do, but I can guarantee you that it won't be [BLANK]." You can fill in that blank with whatever job the person held prior to the pandemic: nursing assistant, waiter, corporate executive, or the like. The challenge, of course, is that companies typically look to hire people with previous experience. Once you realize that candidates with previous experience are no longer looking to work in that field and there's no qualified talent available to apply for your job openings, then the crisis reaction kicks into effect. You can't manufacture widgets, deliver food to tables, or accept new hospital patients if your core employees are gone and there's no one to replace them.

The *Great Resignation* was the term used to describe this massive cultural transformation and disruption. For workers in their fifties and sixties who were nearing retirement but opted to leave and start their own business or retire early, the term *Gray Resignation* was coined. And for workers who were fortunate enough to work through the pandemic but who were exhausted because of massive overtime, double shifts, and seven-day workweeks, "quiet quitting" came into play, meaning workers had reached their "mental max" and drew firm mental lines in the sand about what they would or would not be willing to do for the organization going forward. "I'm not going to kill myself for this company anymore. Life is too short, and I've got to worry about me, my family, and my health. I'm not going to work all this overtime, no matter how much pressure my company puts on me or how few people are available to backfill any of our open jobs" went the reasoning.

The COVID job scarcity, however, simply cracked open the door and shone a sliver of light on what was to come. Demographers, social scientists, and labor economists (a.k.a. "corporate futurists") will tell you that the "population explosion" we've become accustomed to over prior decades—read that as unlimited human capital talent—is coming to a swift end. Think about it: From the time of Christ until the eighteenth century, the world population fluctuated between two hundred and seven hundred million people. By the early 1800s, the planet hit one billion people. Then the Industrial Revolution came onto the scene in the eighteenth century and hit its full stride in America in the 1870s and continued through World

War II. Suddenly, there were three billion humans on the planet. By the 1970s, there were four billion, the 1980s reached five billion, and the late '90s witnessed six billion. By 2011, there were seven billion, and on November 15, 2022, the global population reached eight billion. That means that in the 1970s, there were roughly half as many human beings on the planet as there are today. Now *that's* a population explosion and a dynamic labor pool! But before we discuss engagement and retention, we have to acquire the talent despite today's shortages in industrialized nations, which is where we can pick up our story from a practical standpoint.

WHAT THIS MEANS FOR YOU

First, big job boards like Indeed, CareerBuilder, ZipRecruiter, SimplyHired, Monster, and Dice (for technical IT talent), among others, will likely have challenges identifying the volume of talent needed for tomorrow's many employment openings. While job boards will likely remain "first stops" for companies with job postings, employers are turning to new boutique websites for their recruitment outreach efforts, which likewise serve their diversity and inclusion needs. Boutique job boards like VeteranJobs .net, HireOurHeroes.org, Recruitmilitary.com, DiversityJobs.com, DiversityEmployers.com, LatinoJobs.org, OverFiftyJobs.com, Black Careers.org, AsianHires.com, NativeJobs.org, LGBTjobsite.com, and WeHireWomen.com will likely expand your reach to tap qualified diverse talent. The Department of Labor's Job Accommodation Network (www.dol.gov/agencies/odep/resources/jan) is an excellent source for identifying job candidates with disabilities or special needs.

Likewise, social media sites like LinkedIn will continue to expand their outreach for professional-level candidates. They'll offer functions that allow employers and recruiters to create targeted advertising campaigns designed to reach underrepresented groups. And customized mobile apps and web platforms will permit turnkey employment solutions for smaller companies, including payroll, benefits, workers' compensation, and overall "employment without boundaries." (In other words, workers belonging to the vendor's payroll can work at multiple employers while the vendor remains the constant employer of record.) Technology will continue to provide solutions to labor shortage problems, just as the nature of gig talent and portable benefits takes root in the United States and elsewhere to source talent.

In the future job market, you'll need to be very proactive in recruiting candidates. Placing recruitment ads on a job board and waiting for qualified résumés to appear won't suffice. Your job? Research local resources, such as nursing, hospitality, or tech trade schools and professional development programs, including local training organizations like Workshops for Warriors. Community action agencies, civil rights organizations, and church groups within communities can help employers reach inner-city residents. Further, determine which job boards, social media sites, and web platforms may work best for your organization relative to your geographic location and the types of hires you make. Set your recruitment budget for the next quarter or year by exploring new sources of potential talent providers and funnels. Some will work better than others, but you won't know until you try out different options. Note that a recruitment advertising agency may make total sense as well to help you with your strategic ad placement.

Finally, build a buddy onboarding program to ensure a successful transition for new hires to make it through their first three or six months (where so much turnover typically happens). Talent acquisition and retention remain a living, breathing part of your organizational culture. It also spells your long-term success, as talent remains a company's primary profit lever in the tight labor markets that are sure to follow. Keep in mind that talent acquisition is not a temporary crisis: it will affect your organization's trajectory for years to come, and you—the first-time HR manager—will shepherd your company's most cherished resource—its people.

SPECIAL NOTE: ACCOMMODATING FAMILIES

With parents making up 40 percent of the workforce as of this writing, offering a benefits package that supports employees in different life stages is essential. If your organization offers any particular family-friendly benefits, advertise them broadly in your recruitment advertising campaigns and internal employee referral programs, especially programs that are designed to be mutually advantageous to career-oriented working mothers and their employers. This may include paid parental leave, alternative career paths, extended leave, flextime, job sharing, relaxed dress codes, summer hours, elder care flexibility, and telecommuting. Some organizations provide take-home meals for those working overtime, subsidize babysitting, or offer job-finding assistance for spouses of employees who are relocated. Requiring workers to shut off their mobile devices after hours is another perk that organizations are increasingly giving their employees. All help recipients balance career and family. All square with Gen Y and Gen Z's desires for greater work-life-family balance and harmony. And all help you raise the support you provide to working parents while your employees raise their little ones or care for their elders.

ONBOARDING DONE RIGHT

Organizations are wisely looking to the onboarding and integration of new hires into the corporate family as a much-needed extension to the recruitment and hiring processes. The cost of recruitment and new-hire training is high, talent can be scarce, and ensuring some form of a sheltered or guided transition into the company helps ensure a new hire's success and longevity beyond the initial ninety-day introductory period or one-year anniversary. There are varying and creative ways of establishing a healthy onboarding practice, but whatever form it takes, just ensure that human connection is part of it. (In other words, don't relegate this to an app.)

The questions below can be asked by a member of the human resources department or by the supervisor's supervisor or the department head. It makes most sense for the department director (or supervisor's immediate supervisor) to ask these questions, especially if there are any questions about the immediate supervisor's leadership abilities. Besides, it gives the department director a chance to hear firsthand how the management team is leading, how new hires are made to feel welcome or isolated, how well the systems work, and other key experiences that only a fresh set of eyes can share. But if the immediate supervisor or HR manager opts to conduct these monthly meetings over the first three months of a new hire's employment, that's acceptable as well. Use the questions below as samples of what could and should be asked of new hires during the onboarding experience and make adjustments as needed. The feedback generated from these private, one-on-one meetings provides answers, ensures alignment, and continues to strengthen the bond to the broader organization as a whole. Remember, you won't learn unless you ask.

DAY THIRTY

- What do you like about the position and the company so far? What's been going well? What are the highlights of your experiences so far?
- Tell me what you don't understand about your role or about our organization now that you've had a month to roll up your sleeves and get your hands dirty.
- Have you faced any surprises since joining us?
- Have you and your manager discussed goals and performance metrics?
- What one thing stands out most in terms of capturing your first full month with us?

- Is there anything that you'd consider problematic that you'd like to share with me?
- Is there anything I can do to help you at this point and provide additional support, structure, or direction?

DAY SIXTY

- Do you have enough, too much, or too little time to do your work?
- Do you have access to the appropriate tools and resources? Do you feel you've been trained sufficiently in all aspects of your job to perform at a high level?
- How do you see your position relating to our organization's mission, vision, and values?
- Compare the organization and your role today to how we described them when you initially interviewed with us. Have you experienced any surprises, disappointments, or other aha moments that you're comfortable sharing?
- How has your relationship with your peers developed over the last two months? Have you been made to feel welcome, and do you feel you've made others feel welcome in partnering with you?
- Don't be shy: tell me about some of your accomplishments thus far.
- What else should I be aware of regarding your onboarding experience to date?

DAY NINETY:
SPRINGBOARD TO A QUARTERLY REPORTING MINDSET

While the Day Ninety meeting typically employs a similar set of questions to ensure that the new hire is settling in well and excelling at the role at hand, its purpose lies in launching into the next set of expected feedback intervals: ninety-day quarterly review and individual development plan (IDP) check-ins and coaching windows of opportunity. At the conclusion of the ninety-day check-in meeting, set expectations for future quarterly meetings as follows:

> Let's move forward with the understanding that we'll meet formally once per quarter. I'd like you to schedule time on my calendar for those quarterly update meetings and prepare the agenda for us to discuss, and they're strictly for you to run as you see fit.
>
> I'd like to hear how you're progressing toward your annual goals, if any goals need to be adjusted, whether you require additional support in terms of resources or training, and how your career interests tie into your work. I'll also ask you to focus on your professional development needs when we have our quarterly one-on-ones. Also, let me know if we need to pivot or change direction altogether because of unforeseen changes that come our way. Consider these quarterly touch-base meetings as cornerstones of your annual performance review where everything builds over time so there won't be any surprises along the way. Can you make that commitment to me going forward? [Yes.]
>
> Okay, then, I'll defer to you to schedule the next meeting by adding an invite to my calendar. I won't remind you—I don't feel that's necessary—but want you to stick to this quarterly review program until it's time for your annual review. First, we'll establish our team's goals, and then you can modify them to reflect your own particular performance goals. Here are the types of questions I'll likely ask you at the time:
>
> How are you progressing toward your quarterly and annual goals? Do you see a pivot coming? Will we need to amend your goals?
>
> What would you change or amend in terms of your target goals or timelines to ensure you're remaining on track?
>
> Is any additional training or education required to help you meet your goals?
>
> Do you see any stretch opportunities or areas where you'd like to assume additional responsibilities or gain broader organizational exposure?

How will you plan to strengthen your capabilities in the areas of leadership, communication, and team building?

What can I do to help you meet your goals or otherwise assist you with your own career and professional development?

The end result: better performance, clearer expectations, improved engagement, and ideally, stronger retention. New hires who are engaged in these types of activities from the first day and first quarter will feel a stronger connection to you and your organization over time. They'll feel acknowledged, included, and more excited about their prospects for longer-term success and commitment, so they'll likely demonstrate greater loyalty, productivity, and achievement focus. Don't be surprised to see a superior return on this particular investment in your new hires' futures because of the bonding and trust that develop. What's interesting is that it won't even take much time or effort on your part. Simply make the space for your new hire to establish this new rhythm, and then step out of the way. That's what enlightened leadership and good coaching are all about.

SPECIAL NOTE: "PREBOARDING" AND "EVERBOARDING"

Nothing like a new book to build your business vocabulary! "Preboarding" refers to that liminal period where applicants have accepted your offer but remain in their two-week notice period at their current employer. Stay in touch! Follow up with new hires to see how they're doing in their current transition, invite them to lunch, send them a company gift with your branding to make them feel like part of the team, and keep them excited about the new opportunities that await. (After all, that two-week notice period may provide the current employer an opportunity to extend a counteroffer or appeal to any fears about changing companies.)

Likewise, talent development professionals refer to "everboarding" as a process and practice that turns a onetime event like onboarding into a continuous journey. In other words, even after the first ninety days, the learning doesn't stop. The underlying assumption is that learning is an ongoing process and core organizational value that will benefit a new hire's career and professional development over the long term. It's estimated that new hires pick up, on average, ten new skills in the first eighteen months of employment. As such, the skills needed to perform at the highest levels trump educational credentials for many jobs. In fact, credentialing is fast becoming the upskill method of choice for many employers and workers, especially in light of the skyrocketing costs of higher postsecondary education. Combine that with the fact that American companies are estimated to lose up to $550 billion annually because of disengaged workers, and you can see that talent development, skill building, and employee engagement represent the future of the US workforce and the human resources profession as a whole.

3

TALENT RETENTION
Designing and Implementing Compensation
and Total Rewards Programs

THE WORLD OF TALENT RETENTION, total rewards, and, more specifically, compensation is, as you might expect, huge and changing all the time to meet evolving market conditions and demands. What does it take for companies to identify, attract, and retain great talent? How has the role of compensation changed over time, and where does it currently rank in terms of workers' motives to remain with an organization or look for other opportunities? On a more practical basis, how will you most likely be brought into a decision-making role regarding compensation: starting salaries, annual merit increases, requests for equity adjustments, and the like? What other "total rewards" should you have on your radar screen in terms of talent retention that goes beyond basic compensation?

Clearly, an entire book can be dedicated to a topic this broad, and many of them are available to help dig deeper into executive, sales, team, and other forms of compensation as well as nonfinancial incentives like employee well-being and recognition programs. For our sake, we're going to focus on what you'll need to know about compensation as a recently minted first-time HR manager. No, this won't be enough to make you a compensation guru, but it should be substantial enough to prove your merit with typical compensation issues that are likely to come your way. As usual, we'll start with the basics and expand from there.

THE DIFFERENCE BETWEEN COMPENSATION AND TOTAL REWARDS

First, since compensation and total rewards are typically lumped together, let's discuss what they are and what differences exist between them. Think of compensation as a subset of total rewards. Compensation is the core element within a total rewards framework and includes base salary or wages paid, bonuses, commissions, goal-related incentives, overtime pay, and benefits like health insurance, retirement plans, and paid-time-off programs. "Comp," as it's generally referred to, focuses on the monetary and direct financial elements within an employee's total rewards package.

Total rewards encompass all the elements of compensation and then extend beyond direct monetary rewards. For example, elements or programs within the total rewards portfolio typically include employee recognition programs, work-life-family integration, health-and-wellness programs, workplace flexibility, and opportunities for career and professional development. In essence, total rewards take a more holistic approach that is intended to contribute to greater job satisfaction and overall employee well-being. Next, let's familiarize ourselves with terms that are likely to come your way early on in your tenure as a first-time HR manager.

MERIT INCREASES VERSUS COLAS

Many of your operational, frontline clients may confuse these two terms, so it's important that you can help them understand the difference. "Merit increases" are generally awarded once a year after the completion of the annual performance appraisal process. A merit increase is typically "performance based" and is awarded based on how well an employee has performed in the previous year. For example, an overall performance review rating of "exceptional" or "superior" will likely warrant a higher merit increase than a "meets expectations" or "partially meets performance expectations" score. Merit increases are not guaranteed.

Likewise, merit increases are based on the total merit pool available. For example, a 6 percent total merit pool allocation (and its dollar equivalent for your budget) means that overall compensation will increase by 6 percent company-wide. However, superior performers might get an 8 percent raise, those "meeting expectations" overall might receive 6 percent, and anyone failing to meet performance expectations might not receive any increase at all. In contrast, certain organizations may require that no individual is paid more than the 6 percent allotted for the entire pool. Overall, the purpose of merit increases is to award and incentivize high performance, motivate strong contributors, and retain top talent within your organization.

Unfortunately, too many so-called "merit" systems provide for raises to be granted automatically, almost like a cost-of-living adjustment, or COLA. COLAs are an alternative type of salary adjustment with a different purpose. COLAs are intended to help workers maintain their buying power in light of inflation or changes in the cost of living. COLAs are generally applied uniformly to all employees, not tied to individual performance results. COLAs are often tied to adjustments in the Consumer Price Index (CPI), but depending on an employer's needs and objectives, the Employment Cost Index (ECI) may be a better resource to reflect current labor market conditions.

Rather than evaluating the change in a "market basket of goods and services" that impact the spending habits of the general public as the CPI is designed to do, the ECI focuses on changes in labor costs incurred by employers, including wages, salaries, and benefits and reflects overall compensation trends in the labor market. Further, the ECI might provide more industry-specific data and localized/geographical insights. Both indices are published by the

Bureau of Labor Statistics, but the ECI "cousin" to the CPI offers data and solutions that are much more in line with labor costing strategies. For more on the ECI, visit https://www.bls.gov/eci/. Note that information specialists are available in the national office to provide assistance via email or phone.

EQUITY ADJUSTMENTS

When an employee knocks on your door and wants to speak with you about "getting a raise for all the hard work I do around here," the person is typically referring to what is known as a request for an "equity adjustment." Sometimes born out of frustration based on increasing work volume, sometimes out of perceptions of unfairness or inequity when employees compare themselves to their peers, such requests are often emotional in nature that arrive on your doorstep with an "either pay me or I'm leaving" type of insinuation. Let calmer heads prevail.

First, an equity adjustment may indeed be in line and warranted based on the employee's request. But you can almost guarantee that the employee doesn't understand the nuances behind what they're asking for, and there's a chance that they haven't spoken to their boss about this yet. (That should always be the first question that you ask because it's crucial to gain the boss's insights into how this individual is performing and whether the sponsoring department believes that an equity adjustment is warranted.)

An equity adjustment typically refers to an increase in pay to address disparities or inequalities within an organization. The disparity in question often comes in the form of a perceived unfairness resulting from internal *pay disparities* ("Sally makes more money than I do, but I have more experience than she does and my bachelor's degree"), *market competitiveness* ("My sister makes $5,000 more a year at XYZ Company doing the same job that I have"), and *pay equality* challenges ("Why does it feel like women are paid less than their male counterparts and peers at the director and above level?"). Again, all may be valid points, but it's not uncommon that a perceived inequality may not be an inequality in fact.

Note that equity adjustments are different from performance-based merit increases or cost-of-living adjustments. Equity adjustments focus on rectifying pay disparities. In theory, they're not tied to market conditions or individual performance (although in practice most organizations will shy away from awarding an equity increase to a problematic performer—at least until that individual is able to meet a certain minimum level of performance). Equity adjustments are also not typically awarded for simply doing greater volumes of work. (This is where employees' emotions can really kick in.) Instead, they're typically awarded when an employee assumes new and greater responsibilities. Let's look at an example because this is where the rubber meets the road with employee demands for salary increases.

The employee in question "demands" an increase based on the "new responsibilities" he's taken on since one of his coworkers went out on extended sick leave. You logically ask the employee to (1) make sure his boss is aware that he's speaking with HR about this and (2) put his request in writing outlining the objective business justification to support it. The next day you receive a document from the employee outlining that he is simply doing a higher volume of existing work but not truly assuming additional job responsibilities. That is *not* typically a legitimate justification for an equity adjustment. Adding greater volume to your job is an expectation of employment.

That's very different from taking on new responsibilities. For example, a finance director who now must oversee the accounting staff may be considered to be assuming "new responsibilities." A finance director who now must assume responsibility for supply chain and distribution management is definitely assuming greater responsibilities that might warrant an equity adjustment. But it's important that you understand the difference between simple volume and "real" new responsibilities. Pure increases in volume of the same type of work do not warrant an equity adjustment, although the organization has the discretion to award a salary increase if it so chooses. As an alternative, consider a "spot bonus" or "completion bonus" for temporary upswings in work volume when another member of the team goes on a longer-term leave of absence. This way, the compensation is awarded without being "baked" into the individual's regular rate of pay.

COMP BASICS

There are three generally recognized components of compensation: (1) direct compensation, which encompasses wages and salaries, incentives, bonuses, and commissions; (2) indirect compensation, which comprises the many benefits supplied by employers (think medical, dental, and life insurance as well as paid time off and retirement plans); and (3) nonfinancial compensation, which includes employee recognition programs, work environment, flexible working hours, and the like. Compensation should be managed strategically to ensure a high level of employee satisfaction and engagement while managing costs. After all, payroll can amount to 70 percent of a company's total operating costs and is often an organization's largest expense.

Pay for performance that is linked to organizational objectives is a primary component of most compensation systems. The term *pay for performance* refers to a wide range of compensation options, including merit-based pay, bonuses, commissions, team incentives, and various gainsharing and/or goalsharing programs. (These plans are organizational programs designed to increase productivity and/or lower costs and then share monetary gains with employees based on a mathematical formula that compares baseline performance with actual results during a given time period.) Pay constitutes a quantitative measure of an employee's relative worth. Equity theory is a motivation theory that explains how people perceive the value of their contributions to the workplace relative to their remuneration (which is where things can come off the rails quickly when inequities are identified).

Finally, remember that "pay secrecy" is only a theory. People talk. And they're permitted to discuss pay and other "terms and conditions of employment" relative to legislation passed under the National Labor Relations Act, Equal Pay Act, and other statutes. In fact, policies that specifically prohibit the discussion of wages may in fact be unlawful. Read that: if you overpay a new hire significantly more than existing staff members, you'll end up hiring one person and losing three once they "compare notes" about their pay rates. Don't make the mistake of overpaying new hires because of talent scarcity or acute labor market conditions. Once peers find out how much the new hire is earning, they'll demand more than that (or will likely start a job search). So, if you're going to overpay a new hire relative to other more senior members on the existing team, you're better off awarding the senior team members an equity adjustment first and then extending the offer to the new hire. That's a painful solution, but it's real and can devastate a team if handled incorrectly.

PAY STRUCTURES

There are a few key insights that you'll need to be aware of when it comes to pay grade structures. A typical nonunion salary structure in a hospital might look like page 31.

GRADE	JOB TITLE	LAST NAME	FIRST NAME	CURRENT SALARY	MIN SALARY	MID SALARY	MAX SALARY	COMPA- RATIO
16	Manager, Financial Planning	Johnson	Anthony	143,540	96,250	125,000	153,750	115%
15	Manager, Laboratory	Smith	Ebony	125,600	84,700	110,000	135,000	114%
15	Manager, Admitting	Frankel	Victor	108,550	84,700	110,000	135,000	98%
15	Manager, Facilities	Patel	Anika	88,209	84,700	110,000	135,000	80%
14	Manager, Food Services	Zhao	Rob	81,560	71,995	93,500	115,005	87%

First, notice that the manager classification may appear in more than one grade. In this instance, the majority of managers can be found in grade 15, but higher-level managers are in grade 16 and lower-level managers are in grade 14.

Second, you'll see that the min, mid, and max salary points increase as the pay grades go higher.

Third, the mid salary, or midpoint, typically represents the current market worth of the job. Salary surveys are conducted to determine what the current market value of a particular position is. Always use the midpoint as your anchor when reviewing salary survey data and evaluating a salary structure.

Fourth, the compa-ratio is a calculation of the incumbent's current rate of pay relative to the midpoint (that is, the overall market rate of pay). The compa-ratio range is typically 80–120 percent around the midpoint. It gives you a quick snapshot of how someone is being paid "relative to market" and is often influenced by performance, tenure, or specialty skills (that is, the longer the tenure and the higher the specialty skills, the higher the compa-ratio).

Fifth, many companies "red circle" employees who reach the maximum of the salary range. Employers typically "freeze" these employees' pay until all ranges are shifted upward through market wage adjustments. It's not uncommon, for example, for companies to award red-circled employees a merit increase in a lump sum payment that is not "baked" into their base salary.

Finally, most corporate recruiters prefer to hire below the midpoint of the range. Depending on the job, it can take four to eight years before someone is truly "at market," and while exceptions can be made based on years of experience and specialty area, recruiters tend to use the midpoint as the maximum for recruiting purposes.

In comparison, union "wage scales" are negotiated to achieve increases in "real wages"—wage increases larger than the Consumer Price Index that improve the purchasing power and standard of living of its members. Union wage scales are typically structured in a hospital as follows:

CLASSIFICATION	STEP 1	STEP 2	STEP 3	STEP 4	STEP 5
Licensed Vocational Nurse (LVN)	$25.03	$26.32	$27.49	$28.75	$30.30
Diet Technician	$25.03	$26.32	$27.49	28.75	$30.30
Pharmacy Computer Technician	$22.96	$23.98	$25.05	$26.19	$27.40
Diet Assistant	$19.18	$20.11	$20.97	$21.93	$23.09
Certified Nursing Assistant (CNA)	$17.14	$17.95	$18.70	$19.55	$20.58

First, note that hospital contracts may contain seven or even ten steps rather than five, depending on how the contract is negotiated. Also, all union classifications (positions) will be included in the wage scale. Each step represents a year-over-year increase, meaning that "Step 1" refers to Year 1, "Step 2" refers to Year 2, and the like. The annual increases are negotiated every three years (or however long the current collective bargaining agreement lasts). Once employees reach the maximum of the range (Step 5 in this example), they typically receive the company's general merit increase for that year (for example, 3 percent).

Second, much like a cost-of-living adjustment (COLA), all members receive the same increase, unless disqualified. (Disqualifications may occur if an individual is on a final written warning, for example, but any such language must be included in the union contract to be enforceable.)

Third, employees under this structure may receive two increases per year: one when they move up a step and one when the entire structure is increased to adjust for the cost of living. The first increase is designed to reward the employee for greater knowledge and experience, and the second for inflation. Sometimes those two are combined if the step progress occurs for all employees on the same date.

Fourth, note that union workers tend to have longer tenure than their nonunion counterparts. That's because union workers are less inclined to leave an organization and start at another company at the bottom of the seniority list, which can affect their job security, vacation selection, and other terms and conditions of their employment.

PAY TRANSPARENCY LAWS

Numerous states have passed pay transparency laws that require employers to include pay ranges on all job advertisements and/or that require employers of a certain size to submit annual pay data reports that are broken down by gender, race, and ethnicity. Such "pay transparency laws" are intended to close the racial and gender wage gaps that have traditionally been perpetuated in the external hiring and internal transfer processes.

Let's look at a simple example. Two skilled craftworkers apply for an open position at your organization. The male candidate currently earns $30/hour at his place of employment; the female candidate earns $27/hour at her place of employment. If your compensation practices typically award new hires with a 10–15 percent increase over their current base hourly wage, then the male would be offered $34.50 and the female would be offered $31.05, thus perpetuating the disparity in the wages (despite the fact that they'll be doing the same work and have similar backgrounds and years of experience). The goal of pay transparency laws is to "blind the compensation scales" so that employers pay people what they're worth for the job they'll be doing, without reference to their current or historical rate of pay.

Yes, this makes sense in theory, and it's noble that the federal and state governments are attempting to address a long-standing issue that plagues our workforce. But it makes it difficult to extend salary offers on a practical basis because employers feel like they're shooting in the dark. (Note, however, that it is lawful for employers to ask candidates about their salary expectations during the interviewing process.) It likewise makes it challenging and costly to determine how to adjust current employees' rates of pay. But consider this:

- Pay inequities have long left women and people of color with less buying power, and the gaps are especially pronounced among the disabled, members of the LGBTQ population, and those suffering from what is known as the "motherhood penalty."
- After hovering around 60 percent since the mid-1950s, the ratio of women's to men's median pay began to rise in the late 1970s and reached about 70 percent by 1990.
- Today, on average, women working full-time, year-round are paid 83.7 percent of what men are paid. This inequity is even greater for Black and Hispanic women.
- It will take more than half a century to close the gender pay gap at the historical rate of progress, according to PricewaterhouseCoopers' *Women in Work Index 2023*.
- Equal pay laws are an attempt at ensuring that employers pay men and women equally for substantially similar work. "Pay," in this case, is not just salary but all forms of compensation. This can include overtime, bonuses, profit sharing options, stock options, life and health insurance benefits, travel reimbursements, and vacation and holiday pay.

Gen-Y millennials and Gen-Z Zoomers are particularly focused on diversity of thoughts, ideas, and voices as well as working for an ethical company that cares about them personally. As such, attempts at enhancing improvements in pay gap disparities will likely spread as organizations look to remedy long-term inequities in starting salaries or overall employee compensation. Here's a quick checklist of how to "slot in" candidates relative to your existing employees and make apples-to-apples comparisons of external candidates' starting salaries, especially with high volume positions and classifications, when you're not permitted to ask about historical salary data:

1. Number of years of experience in this particular field or discipline	
2. Number of years of total work experience (i.e., beyond high school or college)	
3. Specialty experience or designations within a particular craft, role, or trade	
4. Professional certification or licensure and education	
5. Internal equity study relative to existing staff (*Most important!*)	
6. Other considerations	

The same goes for internal equity comparisons. When you post salary data, it has the potential of leading to greater scrutiny. Internal employees often surmise that they are being underpaid for what they do, resulting in pay adjustment requests. Seeing the actual range posted may provide them with a new data point to justify their request for a pay increase. For example, if you list the pay range (minimum to midpoint) of a director-level job opening in your organization at $140,000–$185,000 and an incumbent is currently earning only $137,000, you can expect that individual to knock on your door "demanding" a minimum $3,000 increase to be brought to the minimum of the salary range.

The lesson: If you're not currently conducting internal pay audits to look for pay disparities and outliers (often by department), make that a quarterly goal to ensure you can identify key gaps and, more important, identify the delta (gap) in terms of how much it would cost the organization to bring everyone up to competitive pay levels if you were to do so immediately in one fell swoop. Then map out what a "salary plan" might look like to bring those very same people up to market in the following six, twelve, and eighteen months. Even if your organization isn't governed by any type of mandatory pay transparency or equal pay laws, it's important that you're prepared to discuss "organization-wide compensation adjustments" that may be required to recruit and retain talent more effectively.

A FINAL NOTE ABOUT TOTAL REWARDS

Wise employers will look to the priorities of millennials and Zoomers in establishing total rewards, which often go beyond hard dollars. Understand that perks that benefit others or that make this a better world may have a tremendous impact on employee retention and company loyalty. Consider some of the following ideas to round out your total rewards offerings:

- Flexible work arrangements, telecommuting options, parental leave, and even sabbaticals may contribute substantially to employee well-being.
- Vacation or PTO (paid time off) sharing may make sense in terms of allowing staff members to donate their time to help peers in need.
- Installation of recycling receptacles in breakrooms to collect glass and plastics may make for a low-cost motivator that creates a safer world.
- Adopting a charity corporate-wide or implementing an annual "community day" where all staff members get to contribute to a predesignated hospital, school, or charity may do more for employee morale than you might otherwise expect.
- Implementing an employee recognition program or introducing an app that permits coworkers to compliment one another's achievements can provide a healthy lift and build stronger peer-to-peer support.

- Implementing training programs and workshops, mentoring opportunities, and ERGs (employee resource groups) as well as wellness programs and tuition assistance benefits can help employees with their own career advancement and skill enhancement, which may likewise drive greater retention.

The possibilities continue to grow as we change and mature as a society, so research what's hot and trending out there and see if there's a meaningful and not overly expensive way of incorporating these types of programs in-house.

4

EMPLOYEE BENEFITS
Getting the Biggest Bang for Your Buck
with State-of-the-Art Benefits Offerings

BENEFITS REMAIN ONE OF THE MOST important selection criteria that job candidates and employees look for when it comes to joining or remaining with an organization. Organizational culture, work purpose, and the relationship with the immediate manager will always remain critical as well, but those take time to measure; benefit offerings, in comparison, are concrete and reflect an organization's treatment of and concern for its employees. Most people are looking for the whole package—a company culture of learning and professional growth with flexible work conditions as well as cutting-edge, cool work to do—that will keep them motivated over the long term. While no organization could offer all those things to all employees at any given time, employers would be well advised to rethink everything about rewards, including where and how people work and how they build and develop their career. Employees want a new model that's flexible and personal—think "niche health care," "concierge programs," and the like.

What can go wrong? A lot. Overpromising expensive benefits can significantly compromise your organization's cash flow and financial health—that's a no-brainer. And no company will be able to offer all the options and varieties mentioned below, even if you're a Fortune 500 behemoth experiencing the hottest growth in your organization's history. But some of the options and approaches that follow—selected wisely and thoughtfully—can go a long way in expressing your corporate values and the investments that you make in your people.

Worker surveys reveal that dissatisfaction with benefits will likely contribute to job dissatisfaction. Well-being challenges stem from financial (cost-of-living increases and inflation) pressures, mental health struggles, and other factors that contribute to declines in well-being. Living paycheck to paycheck, dipping into retirement savings, and eroding emergency savings and rainy day funds are very real for many Americans and significantly affect mental well-being. As a result, an overall decline in holistic health—incorporating physical, financial, mental, and social health—is the tip of the spear in terms of what your organization might want to focus on.

Workers who fear that their employers aren't doing enough to address their real-life concerns may reason that their employer is tone-deaf to their needs, not sufficiently invested in their personal best interests, or otherwise not doing enough to make their lives better. Want some quick and fairly inexpensive wins in the benefits space? Consider:

- implementing an employee assistance program (that is, a third-party organization that offers work-based intervention programs designed to assist employees in resolving their personal problems, including marital and family counseling, substance abuse treatment, financial wellness tools, mental health care, grief counseling, and legal assistance);
- introducing an Earned Wage Access program, otherwise known as "pay-any-day" plan, which adds a unique benefit to your organization's offerings that costs your company nothing but allows hourly employees to access their pay within fifteen minutes of completing a shift (rather than

waiting for the official "payday") for a nominal fee (for example, $2.95 per transaction). The program typically doesn't require integration with your company's payroll system and has no impact on your organization's cash flow or payroll process; or

- implementing any of a series of apps that focus on mental well-being and awareness, financial wellness, better sleep and health habits, or providing greater peer-to-peer feedback and recognition, which can go a long way in terms of enhancing employee satisfaction and retention. Consider supplementing your core benefits with similar apps a "must have" in your strategic benefits approach, both because of their cost effectiveness and alignment with workers' specific needs.

Bottom line: employees want care. Feeling cared for at work is a key driver of employee wellness. When organizations genuinely demonstrate employee care, they are much more likely to experience higher engagement and productivity. Much depends, therefore, on the perception that workers have of their benefit offerings. And perception is strengthened by company communications and a listening ear. Employers will be best served by considering each element of the employee experience through the lens of care, including purposeful work, work-life-family balance, professional and career development, a social and supportive culture, wellness programs, and to the extent possible, flexibility in where and how the work gets done. A one-size-fits-all approach may no longer serve your organization and may need to be replaced by or augmented with a niche strategy that reflects your working population's needs.

RETHINKING EMPLOYEE
BENEFIT OFFERINGS

What's considered an effective rewards strategy has evolved in recent years. If an organization is going to remain competitive in this space, it must go well beyond traditional benefits package offerings like health and retirement benefits (although they still remain critically important). To remain competitive, organizations need to think long and hard about what current and prospective employees need and value. In the process, they are likely to find that what qualifies as an "employee benefit" is rapidly changing. For example, some employers are expanding the definition of "benefits" to include the tangible and intangible elements of what their company offers, including flexibility regarding where and how employees get their work done. Integrating employee benefits with work-life-family balance needs is a smart strategy, as is offering mental health and well-being benefits (especially for Zoomers, who suffer disproportionately from loneliness, isolation, and depression, which are typically associated with high levels of digital technology consumption).

Parental leave, unlimited vacation, caregiver care, and shared sick leave banks could become foundational game changers, depending on your workforce's makeup and needs. The challenge, of course, lies in finding common ground to meet the needs of a variety of people and generational lifestyles at your organization, including age variations, single parenthood, elder care, educational loan payoffs, and so much more. To the extent possible, emphasize maximizing choice. Build a range of benefits to serve employees where they are in life. For example, some organizations offer a stipend that permits workers to customize their benefits selections by purchasing personalized benefits that might include elder care support, yoga classes and gym membership, telehealth options (especially for mental health access), and pet insurance. And organizations with limited funds can also offer "voluntary" benefit plans that employees pay for but at a reduced rate through payroll deductions.

How do you find out what your employees want and value? You guessed: ask them! Whether you hold focus group meetings or distribute employee engagement questionnaires, take the pulse of where your organization's employees fall in terms of their interests and needs. Compare the feedback found in these surveys with turnover and attrition data to compare notes and build solid goals that connect benefits offerings to retention results. These results may vary by geographic area and even by nation, so depending on how large your organization is, you might need to expand these pulse surveys to touch all corners of the globe.

Likewise, don't be surprised if you're a bit shocked by your findings. Millennials and Zoomers highly value corporate social responsibility and environmentalism. Accordingly, a particularly meaningful benefit might include corporate charitable contributions and paid volunteer days every year. Likewise, you might be able to provide local opportunities to employees who are looking to volunteer but don't know where to begin. In fact, instituting recycling canisters might be a simple and low-cost option to ensure that your employees know that you are listening to them and looking to partner with them in their global improvement efforts. In other words, their "benefits" desires might focus more on others' needs than their own, which is a very healthy sign of their level of self-awareness and selflessness. You won't know until you ask. And the opportunity to stand out among your competition comes from offering customized, targeted benefits that your employees can rally around and make a point of pride.

THE SPECIAL BENEFITS NEEDS OF REMOTE WORKERS
And don't forget the custom needs of remote and hybrid workers. "Whole-person benefits" focus on everything that employees deal with at home, including children, elderly parents, extended family, mental health, pets, and other matters that may be different from that of employees who work fully on-site. Because remote

workers often have unique needs and lifestyles—especially those who work fully remotely or in other states or countries—employers may need to increase flexibility in their benefits. For example, some organizations reimburse workers for the cost of setting up a home office and define those costs very broadly to include ergonomic and computer equipment stipends, sit-stand desks, babysitters, grocery delivery, and even dog walking.

A final note of caution: Many of these benefits sound wonderful, and they may present an excellent return on investment for your benefits' dollar. But, once awarded, they may be difficult to cancel. Employment markets change, booms and recessions impact the need for talent, and so forth. Always look to the broader, longer-term impact of the benefits recommendations that you suggest. Think through whether your recommendations will stand the test of time and work through up and down markets, especially if the investment that you make may be difficult to rescind in the future. With this commonsense balance in mind, you and your senior leadership team can come to realistic decisions about programs that will make the most sense for your employees over the long term.

ANNUAL BENEFITS RENEWALS WITH YOUR INSURANCE BROKER

The meeting or series of meetings that you hold with your insurance broker every year to prepare for the following year's benefit offerings and open enrollment is generally where your organization has the greatest opportunity to balance expenses with unique employee benefit offerings. The following key areas represent the levers where you and your insurance broker have flexibility to affect offerings and costs.

CONTRIBUTION STRATEGY

An employee contribution strategy is how a company chooses to pay for, or reimburse, their employees' health-care coverage. Group health insurance plans, defined contribution health plans (where small businesses allocate fixed monthly allowance amounts by class of employee), and health savings account options should be evaluated relative to their ongoing costs and perceived value.

ELIGIBILITY MANAGEMENT

Hire dates, hours worked, the availability of working spousal benefits, and other qualifications for benefit eligibility are typically explored to determine who may participate in the following year. The goal is to provide benefit and retirement plans that will provide optimal value to your employees and your company while abiding by compliance requirements. It starts first, however, with how you define worker eligibility to participate.

PLAN DESIGN OPTIMIZATION/STEERAGE

Employers need better ways to foster employee commitment and productivity through a well-designed benefit strategy, and that requires using the right combination of retirement and protection benefits. A successful benefit strategy balances attractive benefits while keeping costs in line. The right plan design and the mix of benefits can help drive how employees prepare for retirement, manage health-care costs, and protect themselves financially in case of a disability while helping the company operate within a given budget. Striking the right balance across benefits—such as retirement, disability, critical illness, or accident insurance—captures the spirit of plan design optimization and supports financial wellness and worker productivity.

Likewise, network steerage is the practice of directing employees and members on your benefits plan to in-network doctors, hospitals, and other clinical or diagnostic providers. Otherwise known as *health care navigation and guidance*, steerage occurs when a health plan directs a member to a better or more affordable provider, helping both the employer and employee save money.

LEVERAGING NARROW OR CUSTOM NETWORKS

Narrow networks comprise local, community-based medical providers who are invested in the health of their communities. Providers in these plans have demonstrated their ability to practice and deliver care more efficiently and cost effectively by focusing on health outcomes instead of more services. Also, by encouraging preventive care, narrow networks increase touchpoints with primary care physicians, who become the navigators to specialists.

If an employer wants a more economical premium cost, choosing a plan with a narrow (or "skinny") network may help. Such networks include all specialties, but a smaller network may offer only two orthopedists, for example, while a larger network may offer ten or more. Narrow networks typically reduce premiums, but consumers also benefit from these plans through lower overall out-of-pocket expenses. Note that narrow network plans provide a way to contain costs without sacrificing care, but because they comprise local, community-based medical providers, they tend to be best for an employee population that works at a single location and therefore lives within proximity to the job site or office.

PHARMACY MANAGEMENT

Pharmacy management, as the name implies, focuses on managing and lowering the cost of prescription drugs while allowing workers the most discretion in how they obtain them. For example, pharmacists may recommend using generic medicines rather than high-cost branded alternatives, reducing the cost to the patient and health-care system. Besides generic substitutions, other options that the employer might consider in preparation for open enrollment include cost sharing for copayments and coinsurance, formularies (the list of generic and brand-name prescription drugs covered by a specific health insurance plan), manufacturers' rebates, and mail order service prescriptions.

MEASURING RESULTS:
ANNUAL MEDICAL PROVIDER CHECK-INS

Once a year, it's a good idea to check with your insurance carrier and health-care provider on a "state of the state" comparison of how your employee population is faring health-wise. You'll want to know the following about your plan:

- current number of subscribers (employees)
- current number of members (employees plus family members)
- average age of your employee population versus the carrier's average population
- stability of your subscriber base (which the carrier benefits from in terms of repeat, quasi-guaranteed business)

Check to see how these trends compare year-over-year so that you can celebrate successes, flag health issues of concern, and support any action plans needed to reverse problematic trends. At that point, it's time to get down into the nitty-gritty. Ask the following:

- What percentage of our subscriber population is overweight or obese?
- What percentage self-reports not getting an appropriate amount of regular, physical activity (typically defined as thirty minutes of exercise, five days per week) or sleep?
- What percentage suffers from diabetes or prediabetes?
- What percentage has high cholesterol?
- What percentage has high blood pressure?
- What percentage smokes?

These categories make up the most common chronic conditions that drive the majority of your organization's health-care expenses. Your organization's results may vary, of course, but comparing your results to the insurer's broader population and looking at year-over-year trends and patterns within your employee population are a great place to start. (Self-insurance along with catastrophic coverage may be an optimal strategy for medium to large organizations.)

Next, find out what, if any, new technology may be on the horizon to help plan members (for example, emotional support coaches available via text, apps that relieve anxiety and provide a calming effect, and the like). Finally, prepare your "plan of attack" to address the most common chronic conditions that affect your employee population. Weight loss and smoking cessation programs may make the most sense; walking clubs may be an easy fix with little cost; and incentivizing healthy foods at the in-house cafeteria or campus store may make for a smart investment in your employees' overall health—especially now that you have the numbers to prove it.

Employers pay an average of 30–40 percent of payroll in benefits. Known as the "benefits fringe rate," this percentage divides the cost of benefits by the annual payroll. (The rate is calculated by adding together the annual cost of all benefits and payroll taxes paid and dividing by the annual wages paid.) No matter how you look at it, this number is huge. If payroll is typically the number one or number two largest expense that a company faces when operating, then adding a 30–40 percent fringe rate on top of that creates a number (cost) that will clearly get a lot of attention. Understanding the five levers above will help you ask the right questions at the right time as you prepare for open enrollment to manage costs while providing competitive and sought-after benefits to your workers.

5

PERFORMANCE MANAGEMENT, APPRAISAL, AND DEVELOPING AN ACHIEVEMENT MINDSET

PERFORMANCE MANAGEMENT IS TRULY WHERE the rubber meets the road in today's workplace. It's where employee engagement and motivation meet bottom-line productivity and results. Knowing how to influence employee behavior is a true leadership trait that bears results throughout your career. So, focusing on performance management and leadership development is a smart priority as you enter the HR management ranks and progress into the future—even if your specialty or area of professional interest is not employee relations.

First, a definition: performance management is the process of creating a work environment where people can perform at their highest levels to meet a company's goals. Think of it as an entire work system that stems from an organization's goals, whether that be profitability, a mission or purpose (nonprofit), a particular deliverable (utilities), or health and human services in one form or another (government). Second, a performance management system provides leaders with a concrete framework within which to evaluate employee performance, help align departmental and individual goals with company objectives, build on strengths, address potential weaknesses, and provide guidance to help people excel in their roles and throughout their careers. In essence, you're helping your employees master their craft and leverage their strengths.

ESTABLISHING PERFORMANCE STANDARDS AND DIFFERENTIATING PERFORMANCE RESULTS

Developing an effective performance management system is a logical place for any employer to start, although most organizations realize before too long that it's more difficult than it initially looks. Employees learn at varying rates, process criticism differently, disagree on priorities and the definition of successful results, and worst of all, often work in silos without coordinating their efforts across the team or department. To combat this potential lack of alignment, organizations produce performance standards and value statements to unite teams' efforts and output, typically captured in a job description, developed from a job analysis, and reflected in an employee's job specifications. Performance appraisals are then established to provide team members with incremental feedback (typically annually) to serve as a basis for modifying or changing behavior toward more effective working habits and to provide data to managers about future potential.

Be careful of two potential pitfalls, however: First, "annual" performance reviews aren't nearly enough to provide workers with career feedback and professional development opportunities. Feedback—both in terms of recognition and corrective input— needs to be shared in real time. Further, formal quarterly feedback meetings typically work best as part of the "annual" review. Second, job descriptions are very different from performance reviews when it comes to evaluating individual performance. Think of job descriptions as baseline performance standards and capabilities. Performance reviews, in contrast, should set the bar progressively higher than what's outlined in a job description. The performance review template should consequently reflect excellence so that employees can gauge their performance and conduct relative to the highest, not minimal, standards and expectations. Compare sample Module 1 to Module 2 below for a typical HR assistant role:

MODULE 1
(Core Traditional Descriptors on a Job Description)

Provides prompt, courteous, and professional client communication. Provides timely and well-informed advice to management and staff clients as well as key external stakeholders and vendors. Demonstrates sufficient knowledge of HR services and resources to ensure a high level of client satisfaction. Prioritizes workload based on clients' needs. Regularly points employees to relevant policies. Consistently gains necessary authorizations and approvals for one-off exceptions to policy or practice.

MODULE 2
(Enhanced Expectations in a Performance Review)

Demonstrates total commitment to outstanding client service. Regularly exhibits creativity and flexibility in resolving client issues and consistently exceeds client expectations.

Remains client oriented, flexible, and responsive to last-minute changes in plan. Regularly puts the human relationship above the transaction. Looks always to surprise clients with unanticipated benefits, including shortened delivery time frames and proactive follow-up.

Provides timely feedback in an empathetic and caring way. Tactfully informs clients when their requests cannot be met and escalates matters for further review and approval, as appropriate. Takes pride in building relationships with even the most challenging clients. Enjoys identifying "out-of-the-box" solutions for clients with special needs. Goes beyond client satisfaction by fostering a spirit of loyalty and commitment to the organization, as evidenced by a high rate of recommendations and acknowledgments from even the hardest-to-please clients.

Do you see the difference? What expectations do you have for your employees' performance? Share with your team what higher levels of performance expectations look like. This likewise makes it easier to avoid grade inflation, a cardinal sin in most organizations, where managers score employees higher than they actually deserve. On a scale of 1 to 5, with 5 being highest, the same individual who scored a 5 ("Exceeds Expectations") under Module 1 would only score a 3 ("Meets Expectations") under Module 2 above. In other words, when you raise the bar in terms of performance and behavior expectations by talking about what it looks and feels like, your staff members will gain a clearer understanding of how they'll be evaluated. Your performance appraisal template itself, in this case, can be used as a tool for professional and career development that your staff members can strive to meet. (For more information on redesigning your performance appraisal template to drive individual and organizational change, see my book *The Performance Appraisal Tool Kit*.)

Hopefully, your performance appraisal template will support your efforts in this regard, but even if your current template does not, it's important that you discuss what role-model performance and conduct should look like with your team. Simply hold a staff meeting and state:

Everyone, I called this meeting to discuss how performance review scores will be interpreted going forward. I know we have a simple three-factor scale of Exceeds, Meets, and Fails to Meet Expectations, but let's discuss what role-model performance and conduct look like first and then progress to what you believe Meets and Fails to Meet Expectations might look like. It's important that we're all on the same page in terms of expectations, especially since we're all being measured by these very same factors from our respective bosses. Do we have anyone who'd like to go first in terms of sharing what role-model status might look like in the Exceeds Expectations category?

Of course, job descriptions are important company documents, especially for legal reasons. They establish minimum acceptable performance standards and typically include information relative to ADA (Americans with Disabilities Act) requirements: percentages of time spent standing, sitting, walking, and the like. But if a performance review assesses talent strictly from the perspective of a job description, these "lower" standards tend to be reflected in higher performance scores. After all, who wouldn't "exceed expectations" if the only standards were to "demonstrate sufficient knowledge of company policies and programs" and "provide courteous communication"?

GOAL SETTING

Goals can be set annually or quarterly (or both). Goals are often structured in groups of three as follows:

- company goal(s)
- department goal(s)
- individual goal(s)

You're free to share the company and departmental goals with your staffers so they can think through how they can customize their work to meet those objectives. The individual goal, however, is up to each employee and should be aligned with the person's career and professional development interests, to the extent possible. Set up the individual goal discussion by asking questions like:

- What are you working on and interested in learning more about at this point in your career?

- What gaps can you identify in terms of your current level of skills, knowledge, and abilities relative to your future career growth plans?
- On a scale of 1 to 10, 10 being the best, how well are your personal and professional interests connecting to the work you're doing now on a day-to-day basis?
- On a scale of 1 to 10, how would you grade your overall contributions to the team and the organization in terms of being able to do your best work every day? What can you add or amend and what are you in control of in terms of affecting your assessment here?
- In terms of the Big Three success drivers of leadership, communication, and team building, would you like to focus on developing more muscle in any of these areas, and if so, what might that look like?
- Have you given thought to pursuing educational activities that might help you perform at a higher level here or otherwise broaden your overall career perspective (for example, via licensure, certification, or obtaining a degree)?
- What can I, as your manager, do to help you further your career interests and professional development?

With goals established and customized for each staff member, you can then set the expectation of reviewing progress quarterly. Ask, "What will be the measurable outcomes so that we'll know you'll have achieved your goals?"

Finally, advise your team members to structure SMART goals, with the emphasis on the letter M (which is often the tricky part). SMART goals are:

- Specific
- Measurable
- Achievable
- Realistic (or Relevant)
- Time Bound

It's okay to make a goal a "stretch assignment," extending your staff member's reach into new areas of the HR spectrum of activities. But it's important to ensure that those goals are "measurable." Measurement often falls through the cracks and therefore must be discussed and agreed upon up front. True, not everything can be linked to a quantifiable end result, but the more you can tease out what the end goal will look like in terms of numbers, dollars, percentages, or the like, the better. Similarly, if the goal is to develop stronger team-building skills, a "soft skill" or "emotional intelligence" goal, map out on paper what should result from mastering the goal in terms of relationships with peers, clients, and other stakeholders.

QUARTERLY REVIEWS AND PROFESSIONAL DEVELOPMENT MEETINGS

Quarterly goal assessments can be as simple as setting aside time and making the space once a quarter for team members to share their accomplishments, how they're progressing toward their goals, any potential pivots that may become necessary, where they'd like additional organizational exposure, what licenses or credentials they hope to pursue, and how you can help them in particular ways. Put the burden on your staff members to schedule the one-on-one time with you and develop the agenda. But let them know this is about them—their career and professional development needs and their recommendations to improve systems or relationships at work—and then simply make the time and space to listen and see how you can help. The meetings are for building talent and leadership muscle, codifying achievements, and discussing the individual's needs and accomplishments. Some excellent questions that may help you guide the discussion include:

- What professional or career-related opportunities are you most excited about pursuing? How can we make one of your annual goals about, or build your individual development plan around, what's most significant to you at this point in your career?

- How are you progressing toward your quarterly and annual goals? Do you see a pivot coming? Will we need to amend your goals?
- What would you change in terms of your target goals or timelines to ensure you're remaining on track?
- Is any additional training or education required to help you meet your goals?
- Do you see any stretch opportunities or areas where you'd like to assume additional responsibilities or gain broader organizational exposure?
- How will you plan to strengthen your capabilities in the areas of leadership, communication, and team building?
- What can I do to help you meet your goals or otherwise assist you with your own career and professional development?
- How can you and I partner as coleaders to make things better for the rest of the team?
- How can we quantify your achievements in terms of increasing revenue, decreasing expenses, or saving time? What would that look like in terms of dollars or percentages? How can we figure out how to turn your achievements into bullets on your annual self-review or LinkedIn profile?
- How would you rate your overall job satisfaction on a scale of 1 to 10, with 10 being the highest? How would you grade yourself in terms of doing your best work every day, finding a balance in terms of the company's needs and your own career and personal development interests, and feeling like you're firing on all cylinders in terms of your overall performance? (Follow up with further questions, such as: "Why are you an 8? What would make you a 10?")

Let's pause for a moment, though . . . Do you really have the time to set aside an hour per quarter for each of your direct reports to discuss matters like these? The simple answer is yes. In fact, you won't want to risk missing an opportunity to bond with your employees to help them with their own professional growth and career development—there's no greater return on investment of your time. And yes, there's a risk that you'll open up a can of worms in terms of expectations that you can't fulfill. That's okay, though—just listening and making space for your team members to share their thoughts is likely enough. State limits up front that you can't promise anything, but they'll likely know that already. Further, once you have a greater understanding and appreciation of what your employees want, there may be minor things you can do along the way that make a big difference. Finally, if you manage employees who, by nature, may think more "job" than "career," it's still a good idea to schedule one-on-one time with them. The tone and tenor of the conversation may be different, as will be your questions, but the spirit of what you're doing will always be appreciated.

ANNUAL SELF-REVIEWS AND CREATING AN ACHIEVEMENT MENTALITY

Even if your current employer doesn't engage in employee self-reviews, it's recommendable to use them on your team. Providing employees with opportunities to share input about their performance and goals tends to work a lot better than simply "telling them how they did." Self-reviews can take on many different forms but should focus on three key areas:

1. How well did you perform over the performance appraisal period? How would you grade yourself in the areas of performance, conduct, timeliness, reliability, project

management, customer care, agility, quality, and other factors?

2. How can I, as your supervisor, support you further in terms of providing the appropriate amount of structure, direction, and feedback in order for you to do your best work every day with peace of mind?

3. What are your goals for the upcoming review period, and what will be the measurable outcomes so that you'll know you've reached them?

The most self-motivated employees will provide you with spreadsheets, productivity charts, letters of recommendation from happy clients, and other "bells and whistles" to demonstrate their accomplishments. For those who don't perform this exercise particularly well, that's still okay: your asking about their career and professional development is enough to let them know that you value their education and well-being. Finally, if an employee refuses to conduct their own self-evaluation (stating, for example, that that's your job, not theirs), simply make a note on their annual performance review that you invited them to participate but they opted not to do so. That should be enough to reflect their possible lack of commitment to the company or the role they occupy.

Finally, in terms of fostering an achievement mentality among your team members, consider employing a Quarterly Achievement Calendar or something similar. A simple Excel spreadsheet on the departmental share drive gives everyone an opportunity to map out their projects, including deliverable dates, key stakeholders, and completion acknowledgments. It often creates a healthy sense of competition when employees can document their progress for others to see. It removes any perceptions that certain employees may have that they "do all the work around here." It creates opportunities for greater partnership and sharing, and it makes it easier for you to report your department's status to your boss (especially if your boss needs to cancel your weekly meeting but still wants to know what you're working on). Most important, it gives you a wonderful opportunity to recognize and celebrate achievements grandly, which is such an important element of employee development.

ARE PERFORMANCE APPRAISALS BEING ELIMINATED FROM THE WORKPLACE?

If you've heard about the movement to "abolish performance appraisals," it's probably because of their time-consuming nature, potential for confrontation, and possibility for disagreement between leaders and their team members (resulting in disappointment and demotivation). Instead of performance reviews, goes the argument, software tools and apps can provide ongoing feedback in real time throughout the year rather than only once per year. These may be valid insights, but in reality, this approach sometimes removes the manager's responsibility for providing negative feedback and delegating it to an app. (And let's face it: no app will ever be able to provide true negative feedback to individuals about their performance or conduct.)

Also, keep this in mind: it doesn't have to be an "either/or" decision and should instead be a "both/and" consideration. Performance reviews are excellent accumulation tools to capture ongoing, year-round feedback. After all, what gets measured gets managed, and without a formal cumulative scorecard reflecting an entire year's performance, it becomes difficult to justify exceptions in merit and bonus payouts or justifications for promotion. It's that annual cumulative exercise that keeps frontline leaders and their staff members disciplined and focused, especially when performance reviews are combined with goal-setting modules that tie to employees' professional and career interests.

In short, think about "performance feedback" as an ongoing process throughout the year that results in an annual report or scorecard. Companies want employees to receive current, real-time feedback, immediate recognition, and constructive engagement discussions surrounding their performance and conduct so they can learn and master their craft. So do employees: Gen Y and Gen Z rank career and professional development among their top priorities for joining and remaining with companies. Therefore, have your direct reports schedule time on your calendar quarterly to review their then current progress toward their goals and professional interests. Instruct them that they're responsible for developing the agenda; your job is to serve as a leader and coach to help them achieve their goals. This rhythm of immediate, real-time feedback plus quarterly goal review makes annual performance meetings that much easier. And you'll get consistent high marks from your team and your manager as a strong people developer.

POSTSCRIPT

Organizations that abolished performance reviews over the past ten years got little in return. Even if software programs and apps are available to drive real-time feedback, they don't work if leaders aren't using them to deliver constructive, and sometimes potentially negative, feedback on an ongoing basis. In many cases, organizations reinstated the annual review based on employees' requests to gain more formalized and consistent feedback. Many experts still believe the system is broken and look for ways of replacing annual performance reviews, but think of it this way: publicly traded companies issue 10-Q (quarterly) reports that result in 10-K (annual) reports. This formal rhythm works well for investors and can work just as well for workers. When it comes to career and professional development, goal attainment, and celebration of success, the more you can structure your people leadership program to include multiple intervals and opportunities, the better.

6

EMPLOYEE AND LABOR RELATIONS
Proactive HR Interventions to the Rescue

EMPLOYEE RELATIONS REFERS TO ANY ORGANIZATION'S efforts to create and maintain a positive relationship with its employees. As a subdiscipline within the HR field, it focuses on ongoing support for both employees and management, analyzing job performance patterns and trends, addressing substandard performance or conduct, conducting internal workplace investigations, and resolving ongoing conflict. Labor relations addresses many of those same issues, only within the context of a unionized workforce via its collective bargaining agreement. Likewise, managerial ethics in employee relations is a significant area for the HR business partner to focus on, especially when it comes to codes of conduct and adherence to business conduct statements. (See my book *Workplace Ethics: Mastering Ethical Leadership and Sustaining a Moral Workplace* for more information.)

In short, it's a huge area that often can take years to master. Assuming your new HR manager role is responsible for employee relations, and you don't have much employee relations experience under your belt, this is our opportunity to provide some deep-dive insights that will help you to avoid some of the land mines that may await the unsuspecting practitioner out there. Let's start first with employee relations and then move on to the labor piece.

EMPLOYEE RELATIONS

First and foremost, your primary responsibility to your company in the employee relations space is to insulate the organization from unwanted legal liability to the extent possible. True, employee relations specialists and HR business partners are responsible for balancing the needs of management with those of employees. But you're not really supposed to be a perfect fifty-fifty balance. In my opinion, you're weighted toward the management side of the equation, if only slightly (say, 51–49 percent). Why? Because at the end of the day, your job is to shield your company from employment-related liability, either by avoiding liability altogether or at least significantly mitigating it.

Yes, you must be there for the employees as well. And if you come across as too biased toward management's interests, the employees may not trust you. On the other hand, you're not the union: your job is not to represent employees' interests to a greater degree than your company's interests. To think such a thing would likely be considered naïve. Remember, unions are, by design, 100 percent behind workers. Human resources, in general, and employee relations, in particular, are there to find a balance— whatever is in the best interests of both. But if you come across as too employee friendly, you will likewise alienate the management team at your firm. So, it's not one or the other—it's both. But it leans toward protecting the organization since insulation from legal liability is one of the main reasons your role exists.

Most people, unfortunately, associate employee relations strictly with progressive discipline, workplace investigations, and terminations and layoffs. Those are parts of the employee relations manager's role and responsibilities. But effective employee relations relies on building trust with those you serve—management and staffers alike. There's a bit of a calling in the world of employee relations: you're there to support people when they're vulnerable, whether it be from a potential layoff, termination, or disciplinary matter. You're there to help people when they're being stalked outside of work, when they're facing personal credit problems, when their children get into trouble, or when an alcohol problem affects someone at home that's negatively affecting everyone in the family. You're likewise there to measure trends in employee turnover and elicit suggestions on how to improve the culture, build an internal coaching or mentoring program, or engage in activities that will "turn employees back on" to perform at the highest levels.

That being the case, here are some quick snapshots of traditional employee relations' responsibilities that will fall to you as a first-time HR manager:

- employee onboarding success
- employee engagement and satisfaction, internal coaching, career development pathways (sometimes known as job ladders), performance appraisal, goal setting, and talent management
- workplace investigations (including employee privacy right matters)
- progressive disciplinary interventions, including facilitating much-needed difficult conversations, issuing documented disciplinary action, and structuring terminations and reductions in force (such as layoffs)
- ensuring that wage and hour as well as timekeeping records are maintained accurately, and that meal and rest period rules are enforced uniformly
- conflict resolution actions, including bringing "warring factions" to the peace table
- policy wonk, the go-to person for your organization's rules and guidelines as outlined in employee handbooks, policy and procedure manuals, and codes of conduct (as well as some basic knowledge of employment law)
- insulating the organization from various types of employment-related liability that may stem from

discrimination; harassment, or retaliation complaints; wrongful or constructive discharge claims; wage and hour violations; drug testing and fitness-for-duty or performance-based testing; access to personnel files, leave of absence management, grooming and attire, and workplace romances

How's that sound as a list of interesting, complex, and eclectic topics? Do you think it will keep you busy enough? If you guessed yes, you are correct: books have been written about the legal aspects of human resource management, leadership development, employee coaching, talent management, and other areas, including a number of my own books:

- *101 Tough Conversations to Have with Employees: A Manager's Guide to Performance, Conduct, and Discipline Challenges*
- *101 Sample Write-Ups for Documenting Employee Performance Problems: A Guide to Progressive Discipline and Termination*
- *75 Ways for Managers to Hire, Develop, and Keep Great Employees*
- *Leadership Offense: Mastering Appraisal, Performance, and Professional Development*
- *Leadership Defense: Mastering Progressive Discipline and Structuring Terminations*
- *New Managers: Mastering the "Big 3" Principles of Leadership, Communication, and Team Building*

LABOR RELATIONS

Union organizing in the private sector is on the rise. That's particularly true at small to midsize companies that may never have seen themselves as a union organizer's likely target. But here's the thing—it's not the big players at the large unions who are targeting employers right now. Instead, young Gen-Z workers are taking matters into their own hands and forming microunions consisting of just a few employees at coffee shops, fast-food restaurants, retail stores, and other workplaces.

Regardless of whether you agree with unionization in spirit or philosophy, rest assured that your company will not want to become unionized. And if it's already unionized, it will attempt to retain as much discretion in its operational decision-making as possible. Therefore, regardless of your personal feelings or beliefs about the union movement relative to workers' rights, understand that you firmly stand on the "management" side of the equation (that is, representing the company's best interests) when it comes to labor relations activities. If that doesn't square with you philosophically for whatever reason, you might want to avoid injecting yourself into the labor relations space altogether. Following are some of the highlights of the labor relations field that you'll want to be aware of and focus on as a human resources manager.

UNION ORGANIZING ATTEMPTS

FOE Rights for Managers: There are certain things managers and supervisors can communicate during a union organizing campaign. Follow the FOE rules—Facts, Opinions, and Examples, such as the following:

- Facts—It is legal to share publicly available facts about your company or from the National Labor Relations Act, the website unionfacts.com, and other reputable sources.
- Opinions—It is legal to share why you feel a union is not needed for employees at your work site.
- Examples—It is legal to share real examples and stories of others to highlight why a union is not necessarily in the employees' best interests.

TIPS Limitations for Managers: What managers may *not* do can be conveniently summed up in the acronym TIPS. Managers may not:

- Threaten
- Interrogate
- Promise (benefits for voting against the union)
- Surveil or spy

TIPS are fairly self-explanatory. Logically, you can't threaten to retaliate against anyone who expresses interest in joining a union. You can't grill your employees to find out "who's behind all this, who's driving it, and who's the main voice to the union." While you have the right to speak with your employees about what's ailing them and even attempt to remedy what's broken as part of your normal employee relations program, you can't promise that you'll fix something "if the employees don't go union." And you can't surveil or spy by looking to see what's going on or where and when employee gatherings are occurring to discuss unionization. In short, you can't take any adverse action simply because an employee supports a union, votes to join a union, or participates in any activity deemed "concerted and protected" under the National Labor Relations Act without expecting to be charged with "unlawful discrimination." Further questions should be directed to your labor lawyer for more specific information.

STRIKE OR LOCKOUT PROVISIONS

Contract negotiations happen at specific windows that are predetermined by the language in the collective bargaining agreement. It's not uncommon, for example, for contracts to stipulate that they will remain in place for three years. Then, six months before the three-year expiration date, contract negotiations typically begin.

Note that we're usually talking about basic preparations when we say "begin." It's actually in the union's best interests to delay the start of negotiations so that the contract actually expires at some point during those negotiations. Why? Because once the contract has formally expired, the union then has the right to invoke a strike—that is, an economic weapon used during bargaining to incentivize the company to give into the union's demands. Companies, likewise, have the right to "lock out" union workers in this postcontract expiration period, which means the workers are banned from the company's place of business without pay or benefits for the duration of the lockout period. Sounds pretty intense, doesn't it? Well, it's designed that way.

Expect your organization to provide you with talking points to explain what the company is doing to take countermeasures to a strike or address a lockout. Communications will typically include logistics challenges like:

- formal responses to picket lines and protests
- transportation and access for nonstriking workers to be able to move easily and safely to, in, and between facilities
- human resources planning, including the hiring of temporary workers as strike replacements, protection of nonstriking workers, and redeployment of management into production roles
- regulatory compliance, including reporting and documentation, dealing with many regulatory and government agencies, including police or contracted security on the worksite during a strike or lockout to ensure things don't get out of hand
- supply chain issues, as the purpose of a strike is to stop production and deliverables; contingency planning to address the processes of taking orders, obtaining raw materials, running production, shipping, as well as introducing new suppliers

Finally, be sure to ask specific questions of your labor counsel about what, if anything, may be said to nonstriking employees about the strike or picket line, jeers or threats from coworkers on the other side of the line, and messaging to employees not involved in the strike. True, this is meant to get ugly, but there are few greater opportunities for you to demonstrate exemplary leadership than when under the cloud of a strike or lockout.

UNION DECERTIFICATION PROCESS

Workers can remove a union through *decertification*: the process by which the National Labor Relations Board (NLRB) allows workers to call for a special election to remove the union as their exclusive bargaining representative. What's important for you to remember as a first-time HR manager, though, is that companies or individual managers are not allowed to encourage or assist with decertifying a union. Read that as: stay away and let it play itself out. The effort to decertify must be led entirely by employees. But employees may reach out to other organizations to help, including the National Right to Work Foundation. Likewise, employers may provide "ministerial assistance" (only) to employees for help, meaning they may point out resources where workers can get help. Again, follow the directives of your senior leadership team and labor counsel before attempting to do any of this on your own.

Sample statements that managers, management, and companies may *not* make under any circumstances during the union decertification process include:

- "If you don't like paying unions, consider starting a union decertification campaign."
- "HR will be distributing a union decertification sign-up sheet."

- "If you don't decertify, I'm guessing there will be no merit increases this year."
- "If you decertify, they'll be reinstating the tuition reimbursement program that was negotiated away during bargaining."
- "I've heard that without a decertification vote, they'll be closing this facility."

Warning: such statements may actually invalidate the decertification process.

The objective of decertification is to determine whether a union continues to enjoy "majority status in a bargaining unit." If not, the union's right to represent those workers is terminated. A decertification election is held to test the union's majority status. Once a union is decertified, it no longer has a right to represent workers or to negotiate on their behalf.

Once the petition is properly filed, the NLRB then sets up a secret-ballot election in response to the petition document. The NLRB determines the appropriate group of people to vote in the election. If 50 percent or more of the employees vote against union representation, the union will no longer have representation rights, and the employees will once again be able to deal directly with the company on issues related to pay, benefits, and working conditions. Remember as well that unions cannot prohibit employees from exercising their rights to decertify. If the union tries to pressure employees to stop a decertification effort, it should be reported to the NLRB because such interference is illegal. Note that unions often try to stall a decertification election by filing unfair labor practice charges against the employer. The NLRB will often not hold the election until the charges are resolved. This makes it especially important that the employer follows the law so employees do not lose their opportunity to decertify.

There are numerous technical dos and don'ts that go beyond the scope of this book and are better answered by senior management, in-house counsel, or your external labor attorney, including fil-ing period windows, "showing of interest" petitions, secret bal-lot election rules, and National Labor Relations Board filings, among other things. What you need to remember is that workers can undertake decertification efforts only during nonwork times and in nonwork areas. They cannot use company equipment or resources. And most important—management cannot be involved in any way in this effort.

SPECIAL NOTE:
UNION WORKERS ARE NOT EMPLOYED "AT WILL"

Union workers' terms and conditions of employment are governed by a collective bargaining agreement that requires "cause" for discipline or dis-charge. By definition, therefore, they are not employed "at will." In other words, unlike with at-will employees, a company may not terminate union workers "for any reason or for no reason at all." Instead, the employer must follow the terms of the union contract—in particular, the disciplinary action section of the collective bargaining agreement—before terminating any union members. The union's focus when it comes to disciplinary action and termination will always lie in ensuring that due process was accorded the worker/member, meaning that the individual understood in writing what the problem was, knew what he or she had to do to fix the problem, was given a reasonable amount of time and opportunity to demonstrate improvement, and understood the consequences of inaction.

7

LEARNING AND DEVELOPMENT
Designing and Building a Learning Organization

TRAINING AND DEVELOPMENT (T&D), ALSO KNOWN as learning and development (L&D), is at an interesting inflection point as a corporate tool to develop and grow internal talent. On the one hand, we know that millennials and Zoomers want career and professional development as a top priority; it drives their decisions to join and remain with an employer. Further, according to ChiefLearningOfficer.com, organizations spend more than $366 billion annually on leadership development worldwide. So it's definitely a big business. Yet 75 percent of companies say their leadership programs are not very effective, and only 11 percent report having a strong succession plan to fill critical leadership roles. In addition, more than two-thirds of workers report that the worst part of their lives is their immediate boss. It's clear that traditional leadership development programs aren't working. So what gives? What's broken and how do we fix it? And even more important, how do we reach the gold standard of becoming a "continuous learning organization" that envelops a sense of agility and change management into its culture?

First, we'll assume for this chapter that you didn't rise through the ranks of learning and development to make it to your current HR manager position. If you did, that's great. But since most readers will have come from alternative paths into HR management—recruitment, employee relations, compensation, and the like—we'll approach the training topic from a higher, more holistic level to provide clearer insight into the broader moving pieces. Second, due to rapid changes in technology, the nature of training is changing quickly. Microlearning, just-in-time content customization, and artificial intelligence will change the face of traditional learning exponentially. Finally, no matter what problems you come across, there is likely some training or development element that will help you move the needle forward in terms of workers' KSAIVs—knowledge, skills, abilities, interests, and values—to address whatever shortcomings are in play.

THE DIFFERENCE BETWEEN TRAINING, DEVELOPMENT, AND OD

The traditional approach to customizing training programs lies in

- initiating a training needs assessment;
- designing an appropriate training program;
- determining the optimal training delivery method for implementation; and
- evaluating the effectiveness of the training program.

There are multitudes of books available in the training space that will help you map out how to approach the key steps of instructional design, content delivery, and return on investment. It's important that you understand what these core building blocks are, but it's likewise crucial that you understand the technical differences between training, development, and OD (organizational development).

Training tends to be more narrowly focused and oriented toward enhancing immediate performance, specific tasks, or roles.

Training often conjures up perceptions of new hires learning basic skills to be brought up to speed in a specific job.

Development tends to focus more on broadening an individual's skills for future opportunities (rather than the immediate job) and is more long term in nature. Development builds off a preexisting foundation to improve and accentuate capabilities that focus on leadership, communication, and team building, for example.

Organizational development, or OD, is much broader in nature and is intended to have an organization-wide impact. OD is an effort that focuses on improving an organization's capability through the alignment of strategy, structure, people, rewards, metrics, and management processes. It involves an ongoing, systematic, long-range process of driving organizational effectiveness, solving problems, and improving organizational performance.

Research shows that an organization's revenues and overall profitability are positively correlated to the amount of training it provides its workers. US businesses provide forty-five to fifty-five hours of training annually on average, although this includes programs outside of formal "training" programs, like new hire orientation and onboarding. It also includes required regulatory training in the areas of safety, ethics / codes of conduct, anti-harassment, and the like.

THE CHANGING FACE OF TRAINING OFFERINGS—THE TOOLS AT YOUR FINGERTIPS

Next, with so many new learning and development options at your fingertips, it's important that we inventory what's available to you, depending on the training needs and challenges you're facing. Refer to this grid to identify potential training delivery methodologies that may work best for your workforce.

TRAINING INTERVENTION	PRACTICAL APPLICATIONS AND INSIGHTS
INTERNSHIPS / CO-OPS / CAREERONESTOP	• Internship programs are jointly sponsored by colleges, universities, and employers. They offer students the chance to gain meaningful real-world work experience in addition to college credit and, under certain circumstances, pay. Organizations benefit from student-employees with new ideas and energies who may qualify for full-time employment after graduation. • Cooperative training programs combine practical on-the-job experience with formal classes, often for one semester, and are generally paid. Students get full-time work experience while going to school. Academic credit and pay are awarded for structured job experience. • The federal government and various state governments partner with private employers to sponsor training programs for new and current employees through American Job Centers, a.k.a. CareerOneStop Centers or Workforce Development Centers. Centers are sponsored by the US Department of Labor and Education and help employers find qualified workers, help workers find jobs and explore career planning alternatives, and provide job training. This can be a particularly valuable talent source if you're looking to hire transitioning service members, veterans, and military spouses.
ON-THE-JOB TRAINING / APPRENTICESHIP	• The most common informal method of training employees is via on-the-job training, or OJT. Developing goals and measures for OJT as well as a specific training schedule and periodic evaluations helps ensure that the informal nature of OJT doesn't detract from the overall learning experience. Posttraining follow-up is likewise a good idea to confirm that employees have not forgotten what they learned. • An extension of OJT is apprenticeship training. Most often associated with the skilled trades, apprentices gain instruction and experience implementing new tools and techniques that help them progress to a certified journey-level worker. An apprentice is generally paid 50 percent of a skilled journey worker's wage, and the wage increases at regular intervals as the apprentice's skills increase. Machinists, aviation mechanics, and electricians are examples of typical roles that benefit from apprenticeship training programs.

TRAINING INTERVENTION	PRACTICAL APPLICATIONS AND INSIGHTS
CLASSROOM / LECTURE	• The term *lecture* sounds like the speaker presents for 100 percent of the time while participants passively listen. But skilled presenters know how to spark attendee engagement via app polling, breakout sessions, role-plays, and other techniques. When large amounts of information need to be shared quickly, the classroom setting often works best. • "Coaching skills for leaders," "effective interviewing and onboarding," and "tough conversations and workplace conflict resolution" are typical workshop themes that align leadership teams by ensuring that everyone receives the same message regarding performance and conduct expectations.
E-LEARNING / LEARNING MANAGEMENT SYSTEM (LMS)	• E-learning or virtual training covers a wide variety of electronic applications, including computer-based training, online resources, and social networks. Content can be delivered via the internet, intranet, mobile devices, podcasts, or other virtual spaces. • E-learning increasingly involves the use of a learning management system (LMS), which combines employee assessment tools and resources under one roof. The LMS can help managers assess employees' skills, register them for courses, deliver interactive learning modules directly to employees' desktops or mobile phones, evaluate and track their progress, and determine when they are ready to advance into new roles or responsibilities.
GAMING / SIMULATION	• The "gamification" of learning is rapidly becoming the delivery method of choice for many employees because it combines learning with fun and internal competition. Games typically resemble actual tasks or principles (for example, respect, ethics, conflicts of interest, and the like) required on the job. • Because of the gaming nature of the delivery, employees are more likely to participate in the training, engage with the material, and remember what they learned. Trainees get caught up in the competitive spirit of the game and absorb the lessons more naturally. This works best for millennials and Zoomers, who are more comfortable with electronic media. • Simulations make the most sense when it is impractical to train employees on the actual equipment. Computer

TRAINING INTERVENTION	PRACTICAL APPLICATIONS AND INSIGHTS
GAMING / SIMULATION (CONTINUED)	simulations can help with crisis management and disaster recovery training. Forklift operators use a simulator known as Safe Dock to learn how to drive and manipulate machinery. Airline pilots use flight simulators, and medical students use virtual reality headsets for similar purposes.
JUST-IN-TIME TRAINING / MICROLEARNING	• Just-in-time training, a.k.a. training on demand, is a growing trend that allows employees to access training when and where they need it. Snippets of training content are delivered that can be applied immediately to the job. Just-in-time training is often used for manual labor, sales and customer service, and safety training. • Microlearning refers to training sessions that often take place in very short time frames, typically five minutes or less. For example, drivers who want to learn a foreign language to help them in their jobs can access learning apps between trips. • Just-in-time training and microlearning are examples of "distributed learning" rather than "mass learning" because of their customizable nature.
SPECIAL ASSIGNMENTS ("STRETCH" OPPORTUNITIES)	• Special assignments are a great way to grow and develop talent and build bench strength for succession planning. Stretch opportunities can involve different roles in different areas of the company and even different regions or countries. Job rotation and lateral transfers provide a variety of hands-on work experience. • Special projects, task force participation, and "junior board" assignments give trainees an opportunity to study an organization's newest initiatives and ongoing challenges. Sometimes, however, special assignments can be as simple as leading staff meetings where learners assume responsibility for delineating and fixing problems within their own department.
COACHING / ROLE-PLAYING	• Internal coaching is important for all employees to receive as it builds self-confidence, trust, and loyalty to the manager and the organization. It is growing in popularity as a method to improve learning and development because it is personal in nature and customized to the individual's needs. Coaching flows from manager to subordinate via instruction, feedback, and suggestions for improvement. It naturally takes into account the learner's personal goals and career

TRAINING INTERVENTION	PRACTICAL APPLICATIONS AND INSIGHTS
COACHING / ROLE-PLAYING (CONTINUED)	interests, intertwining them with their career aspirations and on-the-job challenges. It works particularly well for employees who are being groomed for management roles. • A natural extension of coaching is role-playing—playing the roles of others—in terms of negotiation, conflict resolution, and team cooperation. Role-playing helps raise awareness about stakeholders' concerns and natural resistance to change, along with techniques to overcome people's hesitations and reservations about following a new course of action. Computer programs like Virtual Leader from SimuLearn can simulate role-playing, where trainees interact with animated "employees" and are then given feedback on their performance.
SEMINARS / CONFERENCES	• The Society for Human Resource Management, American Management Association, Conference Board, and Center for Creative Leadership offer programs that address specific challenges faced by leaders in a business setting, patterns and trends affecting the future workplace, and global, life-changing leadership development research and solutions for your organization. • Seminars and conferences may be best when an organization's goal focuses on large-scale change. This could include enhancing leadership communication, increasing teamwork across divisions, merging cultures, or developing future talent.
MOOCS	• Massive Open Online Courses (MOOCs) are free online courses for anyone to enroll in. Udemy, Coursera, edX, FutureLearn, and Khan Academy are some of the major MOOC providers, although there are thousands of MOOCs—often created by organizations looking to grow talent by offering software/coding training that learners can master and then use to apply for a job (think Microsoft and Google). • MOOCs range in length from one to sixteen weeks. Autograded quizzes and peer-feedback assignments may be available, although certain elements—for example, graded assignments—may sit behind a paywall. Certificates of completion and nanodegrees may be available for free or for a fee. Although originally created by universities and reserved for academic

TRAINING INTERVENTION	PRACTICAL APPLICATIONS AND INSIGHTS
MOOCS (CONTINUED)	circles, MOOCs have now found their way into the business world. Applying data analytics to marketing, fundamentals of international business, diversity and belonging in businesses and organizations, supply chain design, and best practices for project management success are actual courses available via a simple online search. • MOOC coursework and certification may go a long way in meeting your employees' career and professional development needs while providing outstanding free or low-cost training.

THE IMPACT OF TRAINING ON CULTURE

According to LinkedIn's 2022 *Workplace Learning Report*, "opportunities to learn and grow" are the most highly rated culture drivers worldwide. Ongoing training enriches and enhances your organizational culture. As we shared earlier, labor scarcity will be a dominant factor in twenty-first-century business. Companies will need to build muscle around talent development and "growing their own" rather than simply relying on external talent to fill job openings or build leadership bench strength. Further, change management and agility will remain the hallmarks of highly effective organizations. The ability to pivot on a dime, adopt new technologies, adapt to swiftly changing market conditions, and build technical and soft skills within their ranks will help organizations stand apart from their competition.

Employee development is a key differentiator. It can be difficult to compete for talent, especially if you're a small business that simply cannot offer more money to win over candidates. One way to compete effectively is to model yourself as an organization that prioritizes talent development. This enhances your ability to attract great employees by demonstrating a core commitment to advancement and can help you avoid competing for talent based on compensation alone. Career and professional development remain a top priority for Gen Y and Gen Z, so develop strong training curricula and publicize them broadly, both to external candidates and internal staffers. Build your program around Virgin CEO Richard Branson's philosophy: "Train people well enough so they can leave. Treat them well enough so they don't want to."

Emphasize the lifelong learning revolution in your employee handbooks and posters. Factor in a tuition reimbursement budget if you don't already have one and encourage employees to use those resources for their own professional development. Celebrate individual and team successes and achievements, and try to incorporate some of the following "game changers" that influence organizational culture:

- Build a buddy program where top performers are tapped to sponsor new hires and ensure their success. Buddy programs should be the first step in developing a "hi-po," or high-potential program where emerging leaders are tapped for broader responsibilities and more challenging assignments. Transitions into the workplace with peer partners lower turnover and speed up onboarding. The reward for the buddy can be monetary but can just as easily be recognition.

- Develop a schedule for regular staff meetings—weekly or biweekly—to ensure that everyone is in the loop and aligned with the department's newest priorities. Don't let employees fall into a rut of doing the same job, day in and day out, with no stimulation or challenge. Staff meetings allow the organizational elders to pass down wisdom to the younger generation. Use this opportunity to get everyone on the same page in terms of priorities and goals.

- Teach your employees how to access MOOCs and other free or low-cost resources to reskill and upskill according to the market's changing needs. Set up creative exercises to research the competition and investigate personal career paths using the Bureau of Labor Statistics' *Occupational Outlook Handbook* (www.bls.gov/ooh) and share what they've learned with the rest of the team. Foster a healthy sense of curiosity. Place people into rotational leadership roles where they can teach others what they know best. Little does more to feed the "psychic income" that people rely on in terms of the reward for hard work and commitment than being asked to train others and share their secrets of success.

- Hold lunch-and-learn workshops that highlight different parts of your organization and interview divisional or departmental leaders who can share what they're focusing on, what challenges they face, and what opportunities lie ahead. Invite guest speakers, professors, and authors to join you for occasional motivational boosts that help your managers and employees feel that they're on the cutting edge of new ideas and technology and not treading water career-wise.

- Instruct your staff members to schedule quarterly one-on-one meetings with their managers to discuss progression toward their work goals and anything else related to their career and professional development, including certifications and licensures. The staff members are responsible for scheduling the time on their manager's calendar and preparing the agenda. The manager is then placed into the role of mentor and coach. The glue that binds someone to your organization is the learning curve. Make sure it's fed, publicized, and celebrated.

- Build career tracks to the extent possible. Encourage cross-training and additional pay for multiple areas of expertise. In a plasma processing center, for example, train new hires in three areas: phlebotomy (taking blood), plasma processing (specimen measurement and refrigeration), and quality control. Each additional step includes additional compensation, and once someone obtains all three areas, a special designation or badge can then be awarded and celebrated.

- Look to new technology for reskilling and upskilling efforts. Employees learn differently, and technology offers flexible solutions that workers can control and master.

The Association for Talent Development (www.td.org) defines organizational culture as the sum of the values, beliefs, practices, and behaviors that contribute to the social and psychological environment of an organization. Make learning and achievement a core part of your company values. Celebrate accomplishments openly. Place people into intermittent leadership roles as subject matter experts as well as buddies and community ambassadors. Assign this transition to becoming a lifelong learning organization to a member of your team as a stretch assignment, including the costs involved as you formalize a learning and development budget. You'll likely find the costs are relatively low and the return on investment is stellar. Making training and learning a key part of your shared values and an organizational foundation can hold tremendous opportunities for employers large and small.

THE FUTURE OF LEARNING AND DEVELOPMENT

There are new trends and developments in the L&D space every year, and lately there is an ever-increasing demand for new ways of working and smarter ways of learning. Some of those core trends include becoming skills based, expanding organizational learning boundaries, and customizing and personalizing training opportunities to meet the needs of the learner in real time. The goal, of course, is to become more efficient and agile, prepare for disruption, and to create new strategies for greater alignment within your organization. But the L&D world is on the precipice of evolving in an entirely new direction via artificial intelligence (AI).

AI is revolutionizing talent development. It will increase the efficiency and scalability of learning tools, personalize the learning experience, provide virtual coaching on demand, generate interactive simulations and gamification (including role-playing), and generate personalized learning plans and engagement activities. With the correct amount of input and information entered into a prompt, an individualized learning journey with robust content can be outlined in seconds. Finally, a greater return on investment will be achieved: by quickly creating more customized content, employees can receive the learning they need when they need it as opposed to traditional learning approaches that are often event based and developed in a one-size-fits-all method.

The full analysis of AI in the learning and development space will continue for decades. It's so exciting that we're on the cusp of a whole new field of technology that "learns," can become more intuitive, and that can exhibit more conversational skills, empathy, and critical thinking. It is not without its own risks, however, which include:

- ensuring date privacy and security
- copyright infringement and liability
- bias in AI algorithms
- inaccurate data scrapes from the internet
- ensuring ethical use of AI

Still, as a first-time HR manager, the opportunities ahead to become creators of talent rather than simply consumers of talent will bode well for your organizational culture, the agility and flexibility of your teams to respond to disruption, and your ability to capitalize on talent as the key lever of organizational success.

PART TWO

ADMINISTRATION AND COMPLIANCE

OPENING ADVICE

THIS SECTION OF THE BOOK MAY be what initially interests you least. In reality, it's equally if not more important than the other sections of the book on HR specialties and strategic considerations. Not to make you paranoid, but this isn't where you want to fail. Think of it:

- Your hospital performed well during its survey with The Joint Commission but failed the section on current employee records (licenses, certifications, and other information captured in personnel files).
- The lawsuit depended on the HR manager's contemporaneous investigation notes, but they were lost and couldn't be produced as evidence.
- Time and attendance records were not retained properly, subjecting the organization to a class

action wage-and-hour lawsuit that settled in the
seven-figure range.

Ouch! Any large missteps in these critical areas may stick out
in people's memories when it comes to how your department performed under your leadership. There's no doubt about it: you'll
want to audit your HR practices to ensure that you not only sur-
vive but thrive should you be challenged by unexpected government audits, lawsuits, or similar challenges.

Your goal: make your area of responsibility clean and transparent. Flag any issues that could potentially come back to haunt your
organization in the litigation arena and share that with your boss.
Consider conducting an HR compliance audit to ensure that
you've captured the main areas that a third party would focus on:
I-9s, employment posters, OSHA logs, and much more. Identify
any "single points of failure" within your area that could affect the
entire organization because only one person knows how to perform that function (for example, HRIS or payroll). An audit estab-
lishes a baseline, helps you set clear and achievable goals, and is
an excellent stretch assignment for anyone on your team who
enjoys compliance-related work or wants to gain greater exposure
to the inner workings of your department for their own personal
interests and career development. I highly recommend an audit of
the particular disciplines that you're responsible for as a manager,
whether you conduct it yourself (in conjunction with your boss) or
hire a third party. Make that a quarterly goal and rest easy at night
knowing that you're in control of the key moving blocks that will
keep your department clean and strong.

8

———

LEGAL ASPECTS
OF HR MANAGEMENT
A Foundation and Starting Point

THE LIST OF TOPICS INCLUDED IN an employee-relations or "legal aspects of human resource management" course easily fills a book. But *this* book can't be that detailed due to the time and space constraints involved. Still, there are certain key legal aspects of HR management that you'll want to master, and here's your opportunity to bring yourself up to speed in the varied areas of employment law. Even if employee relations isn't your specialty area, you'll still need a firm understanding of and foundation in US employment law. There's certainly a lot to cover here: discrimination, harassment, worker protection legislation, labor rights, immigration, privacy, genetics, and so much more. As always, we'll address the most significant issues that are likely to come your way. And no, you don't need to go to law school to practice human resource management; however, you won't want to be caught flat-footed when it comes to discussing something that you're expected to know now that you're in the management seat.

First, some key definitions:

- **Discrimination.** Discrimination occurs when you treat an individual differently based on a protected characteristic or classification.

- **Harassment.** Under Title VII of the Civil Rights Act of 1964, harassment is unwelcome or offensive conduct "which is severe or pervasive and creates a hostile work environment." (Note, however, that states may differ from the federal definition by removing the "severe or pervasive" standard in order to make it easier for plaintiffs to file and prove harassment claims.)
- **Retaliation.** Federal law contains prohibitions on retaliation. Title VII, the Age Discrimination in Employment Act (ADEA), the Americans with Disabilities Act (ADA), and the Equal Pay Act (EPA) prohibit retaliation by an employer, employment agency, or labor organization because an individual engaged in protected activity. Protected activity consists of (1) opposing a practice that is unlawful under one of the employment discrimination statutes and (2) filing a charge or testifying, assisting, or participating in an investigation, proceeding, or hearing under any antidiscrimination statute.
- **Disparate Treatment.** Unequal (disparate) treatment discrimination can occur when an employee who belongs to a protected class is treated differently, specifically because of that individual's protected class status. In most cases, an employee will not have direct evidence of disparate treatment (such as a manager admitting that she terminated someone because of the person's race); instead, employees/plaintiffs must prove their case by inference.
- **Disparate Impact.** Unequal (disparate) impact occurs when an employment practice that appears to be neutral on its face actually discriminates against protected classes. If an employee/plaintiff can show that an apparently neutral policy creates a harsher impact on members of a protected class, that policy will be deemed unlawful, unless the employer can demonstrate that the practice is job related and consistent with business necessity.

Second, understand that claims are often influenced by community movements and events happening at the time. For example, the #MeToo movement (gender), Black Lives Matter (race), and COVID-19 pandemic (retaliation and discrimination) have triggered lawsuits in their respective areas because awareness levels within and among those communities are high.

THE MOST COMMON TYPES OF EMPLOYMENT LAWSUITS

Laws are passed to protect workers, which is of course a good thing. But those same laws can then be used by plaintiffs' attorneys as a foundation upon which to bring suit against employers. As such, an overview of the most common types of employment-related litigation is warranted, as follows.

RACIAL DISCRIMINATION

Racial discrimination in employment can occur in a number of ways and circumstances. People of a different race may argue that they were denied employment or promotions, paid less for equal work, or disciplined or terminated based on their race. Additionally, the law prohibits creating or tolerating an environment hostile to workers of a certain race or policies that have a disparate impact on workers of different races.

The Civil Rights Act of 1964 prohibits discrimination in employment based on race or color. To establish employment discrimination, race may not be the only factor at hand in an employer's decision or action. Even if the employer had other, legitimate reasons for making a particular action or decision, plaintiffs could win if they can show that race significantly influenced the employer's decision. Direct or circumstantial evidence can be used to prove race discrimination.

In terms of civil procedure, employees/plaintiffs must file their case with the Equal Employment Opportunity Commission (EEOC) or its state equivalent before filing suit in federal or state court. In either case, the EEOC will dismiss the case or provide the employee with a "right to sue" notice. (Note that the employee can request a right-to-sue letter even if the EEOC chooses to launch its own investigation into the matter.) The employee must file suit within ninety days of receiving the right-to-sue letter to ensure that civil procedure was followed.

There are two types of discrimination claims: intentional and unintentional. Therefore, an employer's motives are the focus of intentional claims, whereas adverse racial effects, or disparate impact, are the focus of unintentional claims. As there are no affirmative defenses to racial discrimination, employers must disprove the discrimination claim itself. In intentional discrimination cases, an employer may argue that the motive involved was not discrimination but some other legitimate business reason that is consistent with its past practices. In cases of unintentional discrimination, employers will typically argue that a practice or policy is necessary for business. Again, these types of claims can be difficult to defend, so be sure to work closely with your in-house counsel and external employment attorney when threats of discrimination show themselves.

NATIONALITY DISCRIMINATION

Nationality discrimination is similar to race and ethnic discrimination because it discriminates against a certain group of people who share some common traits with foreign-born people, even though a person was born in the United States. Nationality discrimination is defined as the unequal or negative treatment of individuals on the basis of their place of birth or country of origin. Simply stated, it is unfair to discriminate against people based on where they are from or what their ethnic background may be. It can include things like treating employees unfavorably because they come from a certain country and/or speak with an accent. Examples of negative impacts in the workplace include denial of employment, assignments to lower-paid positions, missed promotions, and the like.

The EEOC defines race as a person's "biological, ethnic, cultural, or linguistic characteristics." National origin, in comparison, refers to a person being born in another country or having parents who were born in another country. Title VII of the Civil Rights Act prohibits employers from discriminating against employees on the basis of their national origin. In fact, under certain circumstances, employees may also file discrimination complaints based on an employer's treatment of workers who resemble people of foreign countries because they are "perceived as" sharing protected characteristics like race.

Special note: "English only" speaking rules are generally prohibited under the umbrella of national origin discrimination. English-only speaking rules may be permitted under certain circumstances but must be (1) justified by business necessity; (2) narrowly tailored; and (3) made known to employees up front (by tying the need to patient care and safety in hospitals, for example). But while an English-only rule in the workplace may appear to be neutral on its face, it could actually disadvantage some employees and job applicants with limited English skills. Employers generally must try to accommodate the language needs of non–English speaking workers by permitting them to speak the language of their choice during breaks and other nonwork times. The general rule is an employer cannot penalize workers for using one or more languages in the workplace.

But if accommodating employees' language needs would pose an undue hardship on the business, then in some cases, an English-only rule could apply. This is particularly the case when safety is implicated. Most employers limit English-only speaking requirements to the office or shop floor during normal business hours, while permitting foreign languages to be spoken during rest and meal periods. If you feel your organization cannot accommodate this general practice for any particular reason, speak with qualified employment counsel before introducing a policy or communicating anything to your staff members.

GENDER AND SEX DISCRIMINATION

Employment discrimination involves wrongful or different treatment of an employee based on certain characteristics. For instance, it is illegal for an employer to discriminate against an employee due to their age, sex, religion, political affiliation, gender, or other traits. Additionally, it is also considered illegal to treat one group of workers differently or better based on such characteristics. Gender and sex discrimination comes into play when an employee or group of employees is harassed or treated differently because of their sex or gender. Discriminatory behaviors may emanate from managers, supervisors, human resources personnel, or even other coworkers.

Generally speaking, an employer is legally required to maintain a work environment that is free from harassment and retaliation. Harassment that takes place in an employment setting may include acts, such as unwanted sexual advances, sexual conduct, or other verbal or physical actions, that are considered sexual in nature. Thus, an employer may be responsible for harassment if coworkers or supervisors maintain a work environment that is overly sexual or offensive to workers. Additionally, an employer, coworker, or supervisor cannot harass an employee simply because they do not conform to a "typical" gender stereotype. Note as well that an employer is not legally permitted to fire an employee because the individual has filed a discrimination claim against them, even if that claim turns out to be false or untrue under state laws. The law gives every employee a right to file such claims.

Similar to racial discrimination claims, the EEOC will investigate a claim of gender or sex discrimination in order to determine if a violation occurred. If they determine that there was in fact a violation, they provide an appropriate remedy to resolve the situation, which may include reinstatement plus back pay in addition to a mandate that the employer adjust its work-conduct policies.

On the other hand, if the resolution provided by the EEOC is not sufficient to remedy the violation at hand, the employee may be allowed to file a private lawsuit against their employer. In such cases, the EEOC will then send the employee a "Right to Sue Letter," which will allow them to pursue their private legal claims.

RELIGIOUS BELIEF DISCRIMINATION

Religious belief discrimination specifically occurs when an employee is treated differently or less favorably based on their religious preferences. Title VII of the Civil Rights Act of 1964 specifically addresses religious discrimination and applies to employers in the private sector as well as in local, state, and federal government. The following are considered to be religious discrimination:

- First, a belief is not only "religious" because it is the belief of a religious group (Catholic, Jewish, Christian, Muslim, Hindu, and so on). Instead, a belief is religious if it is "held with the strength of traditional religious views." Therefore, be careful: even if an employee doesn't claim association with an established major religion, the "sincerely held beliefs" standard can invoke religious protections.
- Second, religious discrimination can also include neutral rules that have an adverse effect on those who hold certain religious beliefs. Therefore, while a policy or practice might not directly discriminate against a certain religion, an "adverse impact" legal claim may attempt to demonstrate that those who practice a certain religion may be negatively affected and therefore discriminated against.
- Third, there may be a BFOQ (Bona Fide Occupational Qualification) defense that permits employers, for example, to fill certain jobs with people of a certain religion in a way that is not considered discriminatory (for example, a Jewish school having the right to hire only Jewish teachers). But speak with qualified legal counsel before invoking any sort

of BFOQ in your hiring practices, as the law may be littered with exceptions and land mines invisible to the untrained employer's eye.

- Fourth, employers are obligated to accommodate reasonable religious practices so long as the accommodation does not create an undue hardship on the organization. This covers recognition of religious holidays, prayer in the workplace, and dress code (including head coverings and hair or beard limitations).

Philosophical beliefs may be considered religious beliefs for the purposes of religious discrimination. And a "sincerely held belief" does not have to be a core value of a religion to be considered religious: the belief only needs to be held "sincerely" and as strong as any other traditional religious views. Why do I share all these details? Because religious accommodation and discrimination claims are difficult for employers to defend and are very fact specific. Fact-specific analysis, legitimate business need, and whether the requested accommodation places an undue burden on the employer are the key considerations in religious discrimination claims. Potential religious discrimination claims require legal intervention early on. When in doubt, reach out to qualified employment counsel to help you through this.

NOT ALL HARASSMENT IS SEXUAL

Operational leaders don't always realize that harassment comes in many forms, so it's important that you educate your frontline operational management clients on preventing nonsexual harassment. Why? Because this is all alive and well in courthouses throughout the nation. You'll want to be doubly sure that your clients have a firm grasp on this critical employment law topic. Proactively addressing conduct that can give rise to nonsexual, harassment-related discriminatory complaints should be part of your organization's leadership training and employment defense strategies going forward. Following is a short list of issues to grab your attention and raise awareness about how comments that continuously pepper the workplace could give rise to legal action that may be difficult to defend.

DISCRIMINATORY COMMENTS
- discrimination based on presumption ("I'm not Muslim but you assume that I am")
- discrimination by association ("You've made ongoing comments about my husband having multiple sclerosis")
- derogatory comments blaming COVID on certain minority groups or races
- offensive statements about minority outreach activities in recruitment or about equality movements by specific minority groups (for example, formalization of the new Juneteenth holiday)
- Note: discrimination against people of the same race is possible.

AGE
- overall treatment of "high risk" employees (age and pregnancy)
- replacing older employees with substantially younger employees, even if both groups are over forty (Rule of thumb: if there is greater than a ten-year age gap between the two individuals over forty, courts will find that the plaintiff has made an inference of discrimination.)
- mandatory retirement programs at a specific age (except in certain circumstances that could affect safety, for example, with commercial airline pilots)
- disparate impact analysis for reductions in force (which typically occur when companies select individuals for layoff without conducting a peer group analysis of those potentially impacted and reviewing that exercise without

the help of outside counsel). Read that: you will always be best off reviewing any layoff plans with qualified outside counsel before announcing layoffs or reductions in force (especially if the WARN Act may be invoked).

IMMIGRATION/HIRING STATUS

- immigration/citizenship status: refusal to consider valid paperwork as identified in the I-9 form
- "green card only" hiring rules for immigrants
- ancestry or national origin status: note that "Place of Origin" can be a country, a former country, or an ethnic group that is not a country (for example Kurdistan). Examples: calling employees by their Caucasian name rather than their ethnic name; making statements like "Your country needs to be nuked" or other terrorist references.
- disparate impact of criminal background checks on decisions not to hire minority applicants

DISABILITY/MEDICAL CONDITION

- failure to modify someone's job or accommodate work restrictions that allow them to continue working
- failure to engage in the Americans with Disability Act's (ADA's) "interactive process" requirements whenever it comes to workplace restrictions, modified duty, or other accommodations related to medical disabilities— permanent or temporary

Generally speaking, keep the following guidelines in mind:

- When looking at the prospect of taking on a new case, plaintiffs' attorneys must find a link to one of the protected classes afforded under federal law (race, color, religion, sex, national origin, age, disability, genetic information, pregnancy, sexual orientation, and gender identity) and/or the various protections available under state or local law.

- Documentation in the form of progressive discipline typically acts like garlic in keeping the vampires away: plaintiffs' attorneys want cases where there is little if any documentation and where he-said, she-said scenarios prevail since they can be misconstrued easily or otherwise cause confusion (which always works to their and their clients' advantage). Note that, when entering into litigation, ex-workers often have much better documentation—in the form of little black books with dates and times of occurrences and witnesses—than employers do.

- Remember, it's all about the written record: when a written record can stand on its own, plaintiffs' lawyers often pass on the case (since they work on contingency and only make money if they win). When the written record is inconsistent, contradictory, or nonexistent, plaintiffs' attorneys will be much more likely to take on a new case.

Here's how I've always looked at this: getting sued is simply the cost of doing business in corporate America from time to time. What's critically important to me, however, is that I get sued *on my terms*—not theirs. When the documentation is tight and consistent, when my actions were consistent with our organization's past practices, and when multiple witnesses can attest to how fairly an individual was treated, then I'm on solid ground to defend a lawsuit that may come my way. Always partner with your immediate boss when it comes to employee misconduct and performance challenges. Strive to conduct all your employee-relations matters and people practices in a fair and ethical manner, which enhances your organizational culture and your reputation as a leader, while minimizing the downside risk of employment litigation and liability down the road.

9

LEAVE OF ABSENCE
ADMINISTRATION
FMLA, ADA, and Workers' Compensation

SOMETIMES KNOWN AS THE "DEVIL'S TRIANGLE of leave laws," FMLA, the ADA, and workers' compensation make for a challenging environment that many if not all employers have trouble navigating. These leave laws are well intentioned but like many other benefits may be subject to exploitation and abuse by workers and plaintiffs' attorneys alike. Books can be and have been written on each of these three programs, so it's important that we capture the "tip of the spear" in terms of what you should know and be on the lookout for. Again, these are beneficial laws that are desperately needed for those who qualify; however, disability discrimination has become one of the hottest lawsuits in the land, carrying the potential for punitive damages, so we have to proceed with caution.

Educate yourself well in this particular field of employment practices, benefits, and sick and safe leave laws if the leave administrator reports to you or if you're asked to step in and manage open cases. Most important, know when to escalate particular questions to qualified experts in these three respective fields. Let's start with a basic understanding of what these laws and programs are designed to do. We can then approach the topic of leave administration from an integration standpoint, seeing that these programs often overlap and sometimes contradict one another (much to every employer's chagrin).

FMLA, ADA, AND WORKERS' COMPENSATION—KEY CONCEPTS

FMLA

The Family and Medical Leave Act, passed in 1993, is a labor standard and leave law overseen by the Department of Labor. The leave is generally unpaid, although sick leave pay, state disability insurance, and short-term disability policies, when available, may fund a portion of employees' salaries. Under federal regulations, employers with fifty or more workers are covered. Covered workers must be employed for at least twelve months, have worked at least 1,250 hours during the year prior to the start of the leave (the equivalent of 156 days or seven months), and be employed at a worksite where there are fifty or more employees within a seventy-five-mile radius. Therefore, be sure a worker qualifies for FMLA before granting a leave under its provisions. Likewise, look to your state law equivalent of FMLA (for example, the California Family Rights Act) for additional (and often more stringent) guidelines, criteria, and applications.

Generally speaking, full-time employees working five eight-hour shifts per week (forty hours per week) are provided up to twelve workweeks (sixty business days or 480 hours) in a twelve-month period of unpaid, job-protected leave under FMLA for a number of triggering events, including baby bonding with a newborn, adoption or foster care, care for an employee's spouse, child, or parent with a serious health condition, pregnancy-related disability, and other chronic or episodic conditions. Employee may take time off to care for their own serious health condition. Likewise, a worker may take time off to care for a family member or next of kin due to illness or injury that occurred while on active military duty (and in such cases, up to twenty-six weeks of leave is available). The term *other qualifying exigency* refers to mandatory FMLA time off for employees who have family members serving in the armed forces (including the National Guard and Reserves) and who need to participate in childcare and school activities, financial and legal arrangements, counseling in preparation for deployment to a foreign county, or postdeployment rest and recuperation.

A *serious health condition* is generally an illness, injury, impairment, or physical or mental condition that involves (1) an inpatient stay in a hospital, (2) continuing treatment by a health-care provider, and/or (3) a period of incapacity of more than three consecutive calendar days. Note that any period of incapacity due to pregnancy or prenatal care qualifies as a serious medical condition; mental illness resulting from stress or treatment for substance abuse may be considered a serious health condition only if the condition involves inpatient care or continuing treatment. FMLA time off may be taken as a "block" or on an "intermittent" basis in increments of days, hours, or even minutes. (Technically, the employer must allow employees to use FMLA leave in the smallest increment of time that the organization allows for the use of other forms of leave, as long as it is no more than one hour.) Typical serious health conditions include heart attack, stroke, cancer, back injuries, pregnancy (including morning sickness), Alzheimer's disease, diabetes, epilepsy, arthritis, asthma, and pneumonia.

An employer may require a medical certification for an employee's own serious health condition that stipulates the frequency and duration of the time off needed. The medical certification need not identify the serious health condition involved unless the employee consents to do so. Further, if the leave is taken for the employee's spouse, child, or parent, the certification must provide that the serious medical condition warrants participation by the employee. Recertification may be requested after the time period that the health-care provider estimated in the original certification has elapsed but not more frequently than every thirty days.

Finally, reinstatement rights under FMLA are for the "same or equivalent position," meaning to positions with similar pay, benefits, and terms and conditions of employment. An employer may offer an accommodation of light duty to a person returning from an FMLA block leave, for example, but the employer may not require that the employee take it. That being said, an employer can deny reinstatement under FMLA if it can show that the worker would not have been employed at the time of reinstatement because of a layoff or reorganization.

And there's more . . . a lot more. The intricacies of this law, as well as the ones that follow, often require the advice and guidance of experts in the leave of absence space. Just remember that supervisors may be personally liable for FMLA denials or misinterpretations, and damages could include compensation for lost wages, benefits, court costs, and attorneys' fees. Some state leave laws provide for additional measures of damages, such as emotional distress. Read that: unless you're an FMLA guru and point person, know your limits. If this is new to you and the leave administrator now reports to you in your new managerial position, map out your own guidelines and checklists before you approve or sign off on any FMLA requests. And make sure that your boss preapproves anything that has to do with granting FMLA, ADA, or workers' compensation claims and/or time off.

ADA

The Americans with Disabilities Act, or ADA, passed in 1990, applies to employers with fifteen or more workers and is a civil rights–oriented antidiscrimination law administered by the Equal Employment Opportunity Commission (EEOC). The ADA does not merely prohibit discrimination against people with disabilities; it imposes additional affirmative obligations on employers to accommodate the needs of people with disabilities and facilitate their economic independence. As such, the ADA is not a "leave" statute, per se; it is a law intended to bring disabled employees back into the workplace. But a leave of absence may be—and often is—a means of providing a "reasonable accommodation" under the law. Other reasonable accommodations within a job may include special equipment, extended break periods, a modified work schedule, or a transfer. Further, a "qualified individual with a disability" can perform the "essential functions" (that is, fundamental duties) of the job either with or without a reasonable accommodation. That's why job descriptions are so important: they outline the essential functions of the position to avoid the appearance that an employer is merely rationalizing a rejection of an individual with a disability.

The terms above in quotes are subject to legal interpretation and medical provider opinion, of course. Bear in mind, however, that additional time off beyond the twelve weeks provided by the FMLA may be considered a reasonable accommodation under the ADA. And that's where the lines blur as the two laws overlap. In the past, the twelve weeks of FMLA were the extent of the employer's obligation. Then interpretations began to emerge based on case law that leave time in addition to the twelve-week period could be extended if there was a specific return-to-work date (for example, an additional two weeks beyond the initial twelve-week period) and it was for a finite period of brief duration (typically lasting thirty days or less).

Nowadays, plaintiff attorneys argue aggressively that there should be no or few limits to leave time beyond the initial twelve-week period under the FMLA, as a part of the ADA reasonable accommodation process. Still, the law does not require an employer to provide indefinite leaves. Several courts have held that an employer cannot accommodate unpredictable or sporadic absenteeism. How your organization treats this particular matter should be discussed up front with your boss and/or with qualified legal counsel. In short, when it comes to FMLA and ADA interaction issues, you want the highest sources of authority that you can find to help determine your organization's policy interpretations and practices. Then ensure that you have the appropriate approvals to accept an ADA impairment before you begin accommodating one!

Employer defenses to ADA reasonable accommodation requests include determinations that an employee cannot perform the essential functions of the job either with or without a reasonable accommodation; undue hardship (typically financial or operational); and possibly a direct threat of harm to oneself or to others. Those defenses, however, may be difficult to prove and remain subject to legal challenge. Further, the ADA adopts many of the powers, remedies, and procedures set forth in Title VII of the Civil Rights Act, including reinstatement, back pay, and reasonable attorneys' fees. To make matters riskier for employers, the 1991 Civil Rights Act increased remedies to include a right to jury trials and compensatory and punitive damages for willful or intentional violations. Read that: it's well worth your time discussing ADA accommodation requests with your boss, leave of absence specialist, and/or qualified outside legal counsel each step of the way in case administration.

The ADA defines a "qualified individual with a disability" as a person who (1) has a physical or mental impairment that limits "one or more major life activities," (2) has a record of such an impairment, or (3) is *regarded as* having such an impairment (even if the impairment does not in fact exist). An impairment is a "disability" based on whether it substantially limits one or more major life activities by its nature or severity, how long it will last or is expected to last, and its permanent or long-term impact or expected impact.

This "regarded as" element of the law, however, adds an additional burden to its interpretation and practical application. It infers that even if a person does not have a particular disability but is "regarded as" having one, that individual is covered by the act. For example, if an employer incorrectly believes that an applicant who is qualified to perform the job has a learning disability and refuses to hire the individual based on that belief, the employer may violate the ADA. Note as well that the federal ADA may have state equivalents (for example, California's Fair Employment and Housing Act). And the ADA is the first law of its kind to apply to nonemployees as well: job applicants are covered under the act, and employers are required to engage in the ADA interactive process and determine if reasonable accommodations may be available to hire a candidate.

WORKERS' COMPENSATION

Workers' compensation is a no-fault insurance system that is compulsory for most employers and designed to provide benefits to workers injured on the job. Basically, employers give up the right to challenge a claim for a work-related injury, and workers give up the right to sue employers through costly litigation in civil court. Workers' compensation is the "exclusive remedy" for workplace injuries or illnesses. In many states, it applies to organizations with one or more employees and is administered by the state department of workers' compensation (which may fall under the industrial relations or similar department). It generally recognizes five types of workplace-related injuries:

1. specific physical injury
2. cumulative physical injury (for example, repetitive motion)
3. specific mental injury
4. cumulative mental injury (for example, stress and claims of psychiatric injury)
5. mental/physical injury (for example, stress injuries that manifest themselves in physical symptoms, such as gastrointestinal problems or headaches)

Such workplace-related injuries or illnesses must arise in the "course of employment" (COE) or "arise out of the conditions of employment" (AOE). With workers' compensation claims, there is generally both an employment guarantee and position guarantee once a worker is released to return to work.

Before approving a workers' compensation claim, understand that there are again complex considerations to be aware of. Does an employer-employee relationship exist? Did the injury occur within the course of employment or arise out of conditions of employment? Were dangerous or unlawful behaviors involved? (Intoxication plays a role in roughly 10 percent of workplace injuries.) Was the injury intentional or self-inflicted? Was the claim a result of an altercation where the injured party was the physical aggressor, was it a result of horseplay on company premises, or was the injured worker engaged in a felony or commuting to or from work? In such cases or in situations where "good faith personnel actions" are involved, exclusions from workers' compensation coverage may apply. Note that employees sometimes use the same workers' compensation attorney who relies on the initial claimant to "recruit friends," especially for cumulative trauma types of claims. There's not much that your organization may be able to do to challenge such claims, but group settlements may be an option in certain cases.

Most employers offer "modified duty programs," which are temporary in nature and available for employees released back to work with restrictions. The return-to-work form must include any and all work restrictions documented in writing and signed by the treating physician. ADA accommodations may overlap here. The employer may be obligated to return injured employees to work if they are able perform all essential job functions with reasonable accommodation. If the accommodation will not enable employees to perform their essential job functions, then under workers' compensation protocols, the employer may nevertheless decide to return the employee to work in order to perform "light duty."

A light duty program may temporarily relieve the employee of performing certain essential job functions while recovering from injury. If the company is not able to provide modified duty, the employee will generally return to work only when a release to full duty has been obtained from the treating physician. Here again, the employer may be subject to ADA accommodation requirements. Employers should avoid imposing a "100 percent healed" return to work policy, because partially disabled employees may be able to return to work with accommodation. In any event, it is often best to attempt to return workers to the office, shop floor, or other location: even if they're only "folding napkins," they generally benefit from being back at the worksite and socializing again with peers and friends. In fact, the longer that employees remain away from work, the less the chance that they'll ever return. So, get them back on modified duty whenever possible, and consider creating a return-to-work incentive plan, if possible.

Medical benefits for workplace accidents (including rehabilitation), wage-loss benefits for disability, and death benefits for fatalities are available to claimants under the workers' compensation system. "Temporary disability" biweekly payments come into play until a worker receives a return-to-work release or is otherwise deemed ineligible to return to work. "Permanent disability" occurs when a worker is declared "permanent and stationary" and has reached maximum medical improvement, or "MMI status," meaning that the individual has recovered to a point where the condition will not get any better or any worse. "Vocational rehabilitation" and "supplemental job displacement vouchers" may come into play for enrollment in education-related training that permits the return to suitable gainful employment (typically after one year of leave). The employer's obligation to provide vocational rehabilitation typically terminates when the employer offers modified or alternative work that the employee accepts or rejects. Benefits' continuation under COBRA typically comes into play at this point as well.

> ### IMPORTANT NOTE
>
> Employers should usually coordinate workers' compensation time off with FMLA leave. The time that an employee is off work for a work-related injury or illness can also count against the available leave under FMLA. In order to ensure that this is the case, an employer should give the employee written notice that FMLA job protection leave is invoked. Therefore, make it a practice to issue FMLA leave letters to anyone requiring time off under workers' compensation.

Finally, your workers' compensation administrator may have limited time to accept or deny a claim. (In many state jurisdictions, the limit is ninety days.) An injury is presumed to be "compensable" (that is, approved) if it is not rejected or denied within the applicable time period. Employment guarantees (for example, twelve months) and position guarantees (for example, six months) may vary on a case-by-case basis. Note as well that total temporary disability payments may exhaust after a period of time, typically at 104 weeks, after which permanent disability benefits may become available. In all cases, check with your state laws to ensure you have a clear understanding of the timing and reporting requirements involved. As a best practice, ensure that your supervisors are completing a "report of injury" at the time of the event and attempt to identify the root cause of an injury. Proactive safety programs, same-day injury reporting, and effective root-cause analysis all go a long way in ensuring a safe and healthy workplace.

INTEGRATION AND OVERLAP

Here's where things get interesting . . .

- An injured worker taking leave under the workers' compensation system may also trigger FMLA leave. A workers' compensation injury doesn't automatically establish that a worker is protected by the ADA. That being said, injured workers who have not completely healed may be entitled to undergo the ADA "interactive process" to determine if and how they can best return to work via a "reasonable accommodation."

- A serious health condition under FMLA may not qualify as a disability under the ADA. For example, an employee with mumps—clearly a serious health condition—would typically not qualify for protection under the ADA because it doesn't meet the definition of ADA eligibility.
- A disability under the ADA (for example, HIV) might not trigger an FMLA "serious health condition" because the individual may not have any current symptoms that incapacitate that worker or require absences for treatment.

Yes, it's confusing. In fact, it can feel downright mind-boggling. Hence, my recommendation that you proceed with caution before approving or signing off on any FMLA, ADA, or workers' compensation–related accommodations or leaves of absence. But there's a simpler way to capture all of this together, and it bends toward the ADA piece.

First, FMLA is relatively easy to decide based on the clarity of the law and how it was originally written. Because it was intended only for a finite period of time, it was an easier law to codify, apply, and follow. In comparison, workers' compensation can be particularly challenging and has a parlance and ecosystem all its own. You can safely rely on your third-party administrator or workers' compensation attorney for recommendations to help you evaluate claims and proffer settlements to close them out. But these professionals will refrain from offering advice on ADA or FMLA compliance. That being said, the ADA brings all three worlds together because it's the "action driver" in the equation: the ADA interactive *process* demonstrates and tracks your actions to attempt to return the individual to work. In fact, the reasonable accommodation obligation is ongoing: employers must try more than once to accommodate an employee, and a good faith interactive process is an ongoing effort.

The steps you take need to be consistent, timely, and documented. You can apply the ADA interactive process action steps while the FMLA clock continues to run and while the workers' compensation claim is still ongoing. Keep an eye on the repetition in the template in the appendix and include the employee's ongoing signature, initials, and dates to track the progression of the claim. Monitor this living document closely and update it at specific intervals while workers' compensation claims are at hand and underway (which supports your ADA and FMLA documentation efforts as well).

Clean, clear, and to the point, the ADA action worksheet in the appendix documents your company's engagement steps in attempting to return the individual to work, including transfers, reassignments, time-off extensions, physical workplace accommodations, and the like. It captures your affirmative efforts by date and by option considered, all in conjunction with the medical provider's instructions in play at the time. It affirms that the employee received the current list of job openings at each interval to ensure awareness of vacant positions. How often these meetings occur depends on the employee's particular circumstances, of course, but armed with this ADA interactive worksheet, you can successfully engage in the interactive practice while the FMLA clock continues to run and in conjunction with your workers' compensation administrator's claims advice.

10

WORKPLACE SAFETY AND HEALTH, OSHA REGULATIONS, AND EMPLOYEE WELLNESS AND WELL-BEING

THIS TOPIC MAY SEEM A BIT out of your "HR wheelhouse," but when you move into an HR management position, your organization will likely look to you as a key leader in an emergency. Incident command centers, personnel and labor pools, emergency supplies, and employee communication typically fall under HR's purview—even if your organization has a stand-alone facilities or safety department. But workplace safety is more than just crisis leadership. It has to do with employee wellness and well-being, OSHA audits and administrative filings, and other areas that you'll need to know about—either because they're now part of your scope or because you may be responsible for them in someone else's absence. Let's start with the basics of OSHA and then expand to promoting safe work environments and contributing to a culture of safety and well-being.

The Occupational Safety and Health Act was designed to ensure safe and healthy working conditions for all workers. The Occupational Safety and Health Administration (OSHA) falls

under the Department of Labor and sets health and safety standards, ensures that companies and workers comply with them,
and provides safety and health consultation and training, where
needed. Employers establish formal safety programs, and HR
departments typically coordinate the safety communication and
training programs, maintain safety records required by OSHA,
and partner with operational leaders to ensure the program's success. Requirements and goals include making workers aware of
safety procedures and protocols, raising awareness about the need
for safety and security, and providing incentives and rewards for
safe behaviors. It makes sense, therefore, to view your HR manager role as a de facto member of the crisis management team,
which impacts many of the following areas of responsibility:

- understanding and enforcing OSHA standards
- promoting a safe work environment and culture of safety
- investigating and recording accidents
- preparing for workplace emergencies, including workplace
  violence
- communicating wellness and well-being initiatives to
  build better physical and emotional health among
  employees

A quick look at the sober statistics says it all: Nearly fifteen
American workers die on the job each day, totaling more than five
thousand deaths per year. The financial impact of workers' injuries and deaths is roughly $170 billion per year, consisting of wage
and productivity losses, medical costs, administrative expenses,
and more. The leading cause of worker fatalities each year is motor
vehicle crashes. The cost per worker death exceeds $1.2 million.
OSHA's mission and charter, in light of these extraordinary challenges, includes setting and enforcing standards, providing training, outreach, education, and continual improvement. In fact,
OSHA has proven to be exceptionally effective in reducing the
number of injuries resulting in lost work time, the incident rate of

specific injuries such as back, knee, and shoulder problems, and the number of worker deaths.

UNDERSTANDING AND ENFORCING OSHA STANDARDS

Mandatory job safety and health standards govern machinery and equipment, materials, power sources, personal protective clothing and gear, first aid, and administrative requirements (including OSHA postings and public notices). To do so, OSHA is authorized to conduct workplace inspections, issue citations, and impose penalties for noncompliance. Note that OSHA compliance officers are authorized to enter an office, factory, construction site, or plant at reasonable times, inspect and investigate during normal working hours, and inspect all pertinent conditions of workplace safety, including machinery, equipment, devices, and the contents within them. They likewise have the authority and discretion to question privately the owners, managers, operators, and employees at that worksite. (It is wise to confer with legal counsel first, but employers have the right to require compliance officers to obtain an inspection warrant before entering the worksite.)

Citations and penalties for compromised regulations and standards may be issued immediately upon inspection or mailed to the company after the fact. The employer must post a copy of each citation at or near the place of violation for three days or until the violation is abated, whichever is longer. Under the law, OSHA may propose the following penalties:

- *Other-than-serious:* A violation that is unlikely to cause death or material harm. Each penalty could be as low as $100 with a minimum of $0 per violation, although OSHA may propose a penalty of up to $15,625 for each violation depending on the circumstances.

- *Serious:* A violation where death or serious injury could result and where the employer either knew or should have known about its existence. The penalty minimum as of this writing is $1,116. The maximum penalty for serious violations is $156,259.
- *Willful or repeating:* Cases where the employer intentionally or knowingly commits a violation with plain indifference to the law may trigger penalties of up to $156,259 for each violation. If a willful violation results in an employee death, OSHA can assess penalties up to $250,000 for an individual and $500,000 for a corporation, imprisonment up to six months, or both.

Read that: OSHA has teeth. It's not a government agency to be dismissed or ignored. And you wouldn't want an egregious citation or penalty occurring on your watch under any circumstances. Teaching employees to be vigilant, ensuring that they are adequately trained, and constantly communicating your organization's expectations is the healthiest place to start. For more information on OSHA enforcement standards and penalties, see https://www.osha.gov/memos/2022-12-20/2023-annual-adjustments-osha-civil-penalties.

Of special note is the fact that OSHA has the discretion to increase or decrease initial penalties. On the one hand, an employer that demonstrates a good faith effort to remedy a problem could have its penalty adjusted downward. On the other hand, an employer with repeated serious citations can have its initial penalty adjusted upward. OSHA's Severe Violator Enforcement Program (SVEP) identifies employers with serious repeat transgressions and subjects them to higher penalties and multilocation inspections. Once a company is declared an SVEP, it stays on a publicly viewed list for a minimum of three years, making it more difficult to secure loans, retain employees, and maintain a reputable name in the community.

PROMOTING A SAFE WORK ENVIRONMENT
AND CULTURE OF SAFETY

OSHA offers consultation assistance by helping companies identify and correct specific hazards and implement effective workplace safety and health programs. For example, if an employer
proactively engages OSHA consultation services to identify hazardous working conditions and implement corrective measures,
that employer may qualify for a one-year exemption from routine
OSHA inspections. (Nice perk!) In fact, voluntary, cooperative
relationships with OSHA can result in alternatives to traditional
OSHA enforcement procedures. Alliances, strategic partnerships, voluntary protection programs, and Safety and Health
Achievement Recognition Programs can go a long way in establishing a responsible relationship with local EEOC enforcement agencies, and employees and unions can partner together to do much
of the legwork for your company. Consider this "carrot" approach
as a healthy alternative to the "stick" reputation that regulatory
agencies like OSHA often carry.

Employers are required to complete and publicly display an
annual summary of work-related injuries and illnesses. Companies
must also compute their *incident rate*—the number of illnesses
and injuries per one hundred full-time employees during a given
year (calculated by dividing the number of injuries and illnesses
by total hours worked for all employees during that time period).
Further, state right-to-know laws require employers and manufacturers to publicly disclose information to employees about the
toxic and hazardous substances that they could come into contact
with at the worksite and what the health-related risks of those substances are.

Note that employers have the right to know from the OSHA
compliance officer the reason why their workplace is undergoing
investigation. Employers have the legal right to have a company
representative (typically the head of facilities) accompany the

OSHA inspector on premises. OSHA inspectors have the right to access employees' medical and safety records. OSHA's authority to gain access to personally identifiable employee medical information is exercised only after the agency makes a careful determination of its need for this information.

Important: Employers are not required to permit OSHA inspectors on premises for unannounced inspections. Employers are required to keep accurate records of all employee education. Finally, employers do not have the right to know the name of an employee or employees who file a complaint with OSHA. Following these guidelines will provide you with a sound foundation for OSHA investigations that may come your way.

INVESTIGATING AND RECORDING ACCIDENTS

The supervisor and a member of the safety committee should investigate all reported accidents—even minor ones. Formal inspections in cases of accidents or injuries may help determine which factors contributed to the occurrence and which corrections should be made to prevent reoccurrence. Many employers with more than ten employees are required to keep a record of serious work-related injuries and illnesses. (Certain low-risk industries are exempted.) Minor injuries requiring first aid only do not need to be recorded.

OSHA also requires eligible organizations to keep a Log of Work-Related Injuries and Illnesses (OSHA Form 300). All recordable cases must be entered into the log. A "recordable" is any injury or illness that results in death, days away from work, restricted work or transfer to another job, or medical treatment beyond first aid. Loss of consciousness and/or diagnosis of a significant injury or illness by a health-care provider must also be recorded. In fact, any work-related diagnosed cases of cancer, chronic irreversible diseases, fractured or cracked bones or teeth, and punctured eardrums are included as "recordables."

Each year, OSHA Form 300A, Summary of Work-Related Injuries and Illnesses, must be completed and posted in a conspicuous place where employee notices are customarily posted (usually in the HR office). Be sure not to list the name of the injured employee for privacy reasons. Further, employers must report any worker fatality within eight hours and any amputation, loss of an eye, or hospitalization of a worker within twenty-four hours. Of special importance: make sure you know where OSHA-required records are stored, especially the Form 300 and 300A reports. Be able to point to the OSHA poster (OSHA 2203) informing all employees of their rights and responsibilities as well as the state equivalent poster. Finally, if requested, copies of the records must be provided to current and former employees, or their representatives.

PREPARING FOR WORKPLACE EMERGENCIES, INCLUDING WORKPLACE VIOLENCE

According to OSHA, workplace emergencies are unforeseen situations that threaten employees, customers, or the public; disrupt or shut down operations; or cause physical or environmental damage. Emergencies can be natural or human-made and include fires, floods, earthquakes, tornadoes, hurricanes, chemical spills, explosions, radiological accidents, civil disturbances and terrorism, and a whole lot more. OSHA requires companies to have emergency action plans to deal with these kinds of incidents. The emergency action plan must include procedures for reporting a fire or other incident, evacuating facilities, and accounting for employees upon evacuation. It must also include procedures for workers who must remain on premises to keep critical plant operations going as well as triage procedures for employees responsible for rescue and medical support duties. The written plan must be accessible to all employees and placed in a convenient location (often HR), but organizations with ten or fewer workers are permitted to communicate emergency plans verbally.

Crisis management team plans typically include the key roles involved in the incident command center, including the incident commander, safety officer, public information officer, and liaison officer. The five functional areas for management of major incidents include command, operations, planning, logistics, and finance/administration. HR is often tasked with heading up the personnel or labor pool. The crisis management team determines where employees will gather after an emergency, how they will report structural damage and the status of injured employees in their unit, and how workers can be dispatched across the facility or campus to help or make outreach phone calls, as appropriate. Members of the pool can tend to the wounded, dispatch requests for assistance, anchor heavy office equipment, and do whatever else is needed to support recovery efforts. In essence, the pool first ensures that all employees are accounted for; it then turns those "human resources" into "assets" that can help in various ways as specialists or extra sets of hands.

HR's role, then, is to develop recovery plans addressing the safety, welfare, and health of all employees before, during, and after a disaster. HR analyzes current plans after disasters or emergencies to reveal possible emergency prevention opportunities. It provides constant real-time feedback based on reports from employees, it plays a key role in developing action items for future emergencies, and it provides a source of trained and skilled workers that can be utilized at a central point for assignment. Special note: Make sure you have all of your HR teams' cell and home phone numbers plugged into your cell phone. Likewise, keep an up-to-date paper list of all employees' cell and home phone numbers that you can access if electricity goes down.

WORKPLACE VIOLENCE

Unfortunately, no book on human resource management can avoid covering the topic of workplace violence. The body of knowledge on workplace violence is immense; workplace and school shootings have unfortunately become commonplace in our society relative to other advanced nations. OSHA defines workplace violence as follows:

> Workplace violence is violence or the threat of violence against workers. It can occur at or outside the workplace and can range from threats and verbal abuse to physical assaults and homicide and remains one of the leading causes of job-related deaths.

However it manifests itself, the hard reality is that some two million American workers are victims of workplace violence each year, and some are at increased risk due to the nature of the work they do. Worker-on-worker violence and violence from personal relationships occurring on the jobsite remain a critical concern for employers, but many cases likely go unreported, lessening our true understanding of the significance of this threat.

To mitigate such safety risks, employers should establish a zero-tolerance policy toward workplace violence against or by their employees and communicate the message vigorously. As an immediate second step, employers should establish a workplace violence prevention program, which complements its safety and accident prevention program. The violence prevention program should be communicated via the employee handbook, a manual of standard operating procedures, and posters and other vehicles.

Third, employers are wise to provide safety education and training for workers, so they know what conduct is not acceptable, what to do if they witness or are subjected to workplace violence, and how to protect themselves in emergency situations. For more information on this timely and important subject, please see OSHA's comprehensive resources at https://www.osha.gov/workplace-violence.

EMPLOYEE WELLNESS PROGRAMS AND WELL-BEING INITIATIVES BUILD BETTER PHYSICAL AND EMOTIONAL HEALTH AMONG EMPLOYEES

Job stress and burnout are generally high among American workers. Gen-Z Zoomers—the youngest generation in the workplace as of this writing and born between 1997 and 2012—continue to test out as the most lonely, isolated, and depressed generation on the planet. Obesity, high blood pressure, cholesterol, and diabetes plague US workers' health and significantly increase health-care costs to employers. Crises seem to abound outside the workplace at unprecedented rates, whether it be global warming, war, terrorism, politics, gun violence, and more, making it difficult for the average worker to leave their personal concerns at home.

As a result, along with improving working conditions that may be hazardous to employee health and safety, many employers look to address employee wellness and well-being proactively. Creating and sustaining a "culture of well-being" can include implementing fitness, nutrition, weight management, health screenings, and ergonomics improvements. Some worksites offer walking clubs, yoga, meditation, and even subsidized full-service fitness centers. Healthy lunch and snack programs, gratitude walls (where employees post what they're thankful for), and gym discounts are all meaningful ways of communicating to employees that their organization cares about them. Likewise, remote work, flexible work schedules, and family-friendly benefits can go a long way in helping workers cope with the pressures of modern-day life (for example, "sandwich generations" that must care for children and parents simultaneously) and achieve a better handle on work-life-family balance matters. Such interventions positively affect employee morale and job satisfaction, potentially optimizing performance and productivity.

The National Wellness Institute promotes Six Dimensions of Wellness: emotional, occupational, physical, social, intellectual, and spiritual. Addressing all six dimensions of wellness in employees' lives builds a holistic sense of well-being and fulfillment. Internal mentorship and buddy and community ambassador programs can go a long way in helping employees feel that their career and professional development needs are being met. And don't forget the importance of allowing employees to donate their time, money, and expertise to help others. Instituting annual community service days, adopting a charity that your entire company can sponsor, visiting retirement homes over the holidays to sing carols, and engaging in "bring your child to work day" programs may not cost much but can go a long way in helping employees fall in love with your company while finding a new purpose in their lives.

11

WORKPLACE INVESTIGATIONS FROM START TO FINISH
Employee Rights and Due Process

DEPARTMENTS COME UNDER INVESTIGATION FROM TIME to time. An anonymous complaint, hot-line tip, allegation against a coworker or manager, and the like are not all that uncommon. How you handle the matter as an HR manager is critical to an investigation's successful outcome. Even more important, misbehavior or inappropriate conduct during a formal workplace investigation tends to result in serious consequences for anyone who runs afoul of the guidelines and expectations that corporate HR or legal departments have in place for how internal investigations are to be handled. The challenge? You're somehow expected to "know this stuff" intuitively, even if you've never been trained on it before. Hence, the value of this portion of the book because there's actually a lot to know.

WORKPLACE INVESTIGATION DOS AND DON'TS

The first rule is the most critical: frontline, operational managers who are accused of wrongdoing are not permitted to conduct their own mini-investigations into the complaint. Make sure they know that right from the start. In other words, particularly if the allegations are against them personally, they may not under any circumstances attempt to find out who's saying what to the investigators (HR). Conducting mini-investigations is a serious code of conduct (that is, ethical) infraction that could result in immediate dismissal from employment.

Investigators, by definition, must be neutral finders of fact and must be guided by an attorney to keep the investigation privileged. Any appearance of a manager unduly influencing the results of an investigation or discussing confidential matters with other employees without authorization to do so may subject that manager to disciplinary action and even termination for violating the company's investigation policy, processes, and directives and for jeopardizing the credibility of the entire investigation. Ouch! This is not a place for errors or assumptions. Likewise, you—the investigator—have the discretion to instruct an accused manager to work remotely on the day of your investigation to ensure that witnesses' responses are not in any way influenced by the mere presence of the accused manager.

Second, take good notes of everything the accusers, accused, and witnesses tell you at the outset of and throughout the investigation. Include chronological entries in your handwritten notes like this:

January 15, 20XX
3:45–4:30 p.m.

John Doe asked to meet with me unexpectedly and without a prior appointment to discuss the following:
     What John wants or would like to see happen:
     Next steps:

The way you structure your notes should be transparent and consistent to anyone reviewing your written records. Remember that the notes themselves could potentially be examined as evidence to demonstrate the "real-time" development of the case in terms of its fact-finding process and affirmation that the employer undertook a fair, impartial, timely, and thorough investigation of the allegations.

EMPLOYING THE ATTORNEY-CLIENT PRIVILEGE CORRECTLY

Third, when asked to respond to questions about an investigation in writing as part of an investigation conducted by your company's internal or external counsel, use the "Privileged and Confidential—Attorney-Client Privileged Communication" heading in your email subject line. Here's how it works: Attorney-client privilege is a method of keeping an investigation confidential and privileged. If the investigation is not privileged, then the investigation and all of the communication created in the course of the investigation are "discoverable," meaning that a plaintiff's attorney looking to sue your organization can access the information and disclose it in a court of law. Instead, you want to prevent that from happening, whenever possible, by keeping the communication privileged between the company and the company's attorney. Marking the communication "Attorney-Client Privileged" is one way to help preserve it.

Likewise, limit the communication to your attorney and those individuals your attorney authorizes you to talk to. If you include a dozen people in the email correspondence, for example, a plaintiff's attorney could argue that it wasn't ever intended to be "privileged" or "confidential" since you copied so many people. Instead, your defense lawyer may instruct you to "send it only to me" or "send it to me and copy your CEO." It makes the most sense, therefore, to discuss this with your outside counsel *before* sending any communication their way.

Write "Privileged and Confidential—Attorney-Client Privileged Communication" at the top of your email in bold print, even though you've already written this in the subject line. Yes, it seems a bit redundant, but the duplication doesn't hurt: these documents can be rifled through during a deposition, for example, and you'll want to make sure that the demarcation is easy to see and difficult to miss. Finally, ask your defense attorney/recipient for legal advice and recommendations in the body of your communication (such as, "Please let me know what you'd recommend after analyzing and evaluating this new information").

Note that the privilege works only if an attorney is included and is providing legal advice in the communication; in other words, you cannot invoke the attorney-client privilege by simply writing to your boss (who is not an attorney) and marking the communication "Attorney-Client Privileged." Further, understand that judges may allow or deny requests to keep documents privileged, and the company may, at some later point, agree to waive the attorney-client privilege. Therefore, always assume that what you write could be discoverable by a plaintiff's attorney and shared with a jury at some point during the litigation process. When in doubt, pick up the phone and call your employment attorney first (that is, the recipient of your email) with questions before clicking the SEND button.

A SAMPLE CHECKLIST TO GUIDE INTERNAL INVESTIGATIONS

The main goal of any investigation is to provide a sound, factual basis for a decision by management. The investigation should also produce reliable documentation that can be used to support management actions. Finally, an investigation should reveal whether any misconduct has occurred, identify (or exonerate) specific employees who are suspected or guilty of misconduct, and put a stop to further wrongful actions.

There are ten key steps to launching and concluding a sound investigation, and remember: even if employee relations isn't in your background, you'll be responsible for jumping in and handling investigations as an HR manager.

STEP 1: INTERVIEW THE COMPLAINANT

When interviewing the complainant, take careful notes. Listen attentively. Ask qualifying questions. And document the complainant's accusations as carefully as possible. As you near the conclusion of the initial meeting, always ask, "What would you like to see happen as a result of this investigation?" Further, ask if there are any witnesses who can corroborate the complainant's allegations and be sure to interview them. Even if an employee-witness is off that day, out sick, or on vacation, showing that you attempted to interview everyone identified by the complainant is an important record to establish. (In fact, if you could hold off on concluding the investigation until all witnesses are interviewed, that would be ideal.)

Note: You can never promise a witness absolute confidentiality regarding the information being shared with you. Let the witness know that the company will do its utmost to protect their privacy. But absolute confidentiality cannot be guaranteed, especially should a matter proceed to arbitration or litigation.

STEP 2: GATHER AND REVIEW RELEVANT DATA

When gathering and reviewing relevant data, review the employee handbook, policy and procedure manual, and union contract (if applicable). HR managers often rush to complete an investigation but fail to examine what the policy says. Make sure you have that relevant documentation on hand when bringing your case to your supervisor or to in-house counsel: "What does our policy say?" is typically the first question you'll be asked.

STEP 3: PLAN YOUR INVESTIGATION

When planning your investigation, you'll have to decide if you should interview the accused first or last. Selecting the order of interviews is an important part of the decision-making process. It sometimes makes the most sense to hear from the accused right after speaking with the complainant; however, there can be times when multiple witnesses may ask to speak with you, and it makes more sense to hear them out to have a fuller picture of the accusations at hand. This way, when you ultimately meet with the accused, you'll have a broader understanding of the totality of circumstances involved. Likewise, you have the discretion to place the accused on investigatory leave with pay or ask that individual to work remotely so you can conduct your interview without any undue influence from that person (especially if that person is a team manager or supervisor). As in all cases, keep your boss informed and ensure that you get appropriate sign-off to make sure that you are conducting the investigation—and the order of interviews—correctly.

STEP 4: DEVELOP APPROPRIATE QUESTIONS

When it comes to developing appropriate questions, follow the who-what-where-when-why-how paradigm to help ensure that you understand the full picture. You can then customize questions based on each witness's unique perspective.

STEP 5: INTERVIEW WITNESSES

When interviewing witnesses, remember to inform people that you're meeting with them because they "may have witnessed" or "were reported to have witnessed" something. You don't want your witnesses to feel like they're in trouble or have to defend themselves.

Good faith workplace investigations require employee/witness participation. You may have to remind employees about their obligations to participate. Supervisors must cooperate with the company's investigation, and their failure to do so could lead to disciplinary action. But nonsupervisors may have additional rights under the National Labor Relations Act. Therefore, their refusal to participate in an investigation may be protected by law. That said, nonsupervisors should be encouraged to participate in the investigation.

Again, if your client managers are accused of any potential wrongdoing or inappropriate workplace conduct, they must not "conduct their own investigation" due to the inherent conflict of interest involved. Further, their digging in to learn "who said what about them" can inadvertently establish a record of retaliation should some adverse action be taken against the employee at a later date. In short, HR conducts investigations—not department heads or operational managers.

Special note about union employees: The National Labor Relations Act and some union contracts allow an employee to request the presence of a union steward during investigatory meetings with management that could potentially result in some form of adverse action against that individual, like discipline, termination, or layoff. Union contracts do not typically state that an employee-witness who is not being investigated for discipline has the right to a steward's presence during an investigation. Still, each contract is different, so check on that language before requesting a meeting with a witness who is also a union member. Further, even if the contract does not require that management permits the employee-witness to have a steward present, it might make sense under certain circumstances for you to allow it. When in doubt, check with qualified labor counsel before beginning the witness interviews.

STEP 6: CONDUCT A COMPREHENSIVE REVIEW OF YOUR INTERVIEW NOTES AND OTHER DOCUMENTS

While you're conducting complainant, accused, and witness interviews and preparing for next steps, be sure to constantly review your notes. I know this sounds like a given, but there are sometimes so many witnesses involved that it's difficult to track who said what. Further, it's okay to use quotation marks for particular statements, and it's likewise allowable to reflect witness comments in a general sentence without any quotation marks. But if you opt to insert quotations, be sure you have them word for word. Cases often hinge on what one particular person said, and if you have quotation marks around the comment, it makes for much stronger evidence. Therefore, use quotations sparingly in general unless you have the exact words captured. Likewise, you can ask the witness, "Is it okay for me to use quotation marks around the exact statement that you just made, namely . . . ?" In other words, call attention to quotes and ensure witnesses are aware you're using their statements as exact quotes when plausible. (Some companies prefer witness statements to be in writing for that reason.)

STEP 7: REVIEW AND ASSESS DOCUMENTATION TO ENSURE A SOLID RECORD

Your investigator notes are typically subject to subpoena by opposing counsel if your investigation results in termination or some other adverse action that is being challenged. Your defense attorney has the right to redact notes (that is, remove certain sentences or paragraphs from legal discovery), but that goes beyond the scope of this book. What you want to make sure to do, however, is to review your notes carefully after each interview is concluded. Whether you write by hand on a yellow pad or type notes on your computer while the witness is talking, it makes sense to read your notes back to the witness to ensure clarity. In certain instances, it could likewise make sense for a witness to sign off on your documentation of the conversation so that the individual's testimony can't change later down the road. Again, check with your boss, in-house attorney, or outside defense counsel to see how they would like the witness notes recorded.

You also have the obligation as an investigator to assess a witness's credibility. For example, you may make note of the witness's demeanor and body language, their immediate response to the allegations shared, the individual's forthcomingness in participating and responding to your questions, whether their version of the facts is consistent with other evidence or otherwise plausible, and the like. Evaluating credibility of witnesses is one reason why meeting with witnesses face-to-face or via a high-technology videoconference is key. You may also make note of anything in the witness's history that would support or harm their credibility (for example, the individual won the Employee of the Year Award last year or the witness was issued a final written warning for lying to management on a previous occasion).

STEP 8: AGREEMENT/APPROVAL FROM MANAGEMENT AND/OR LEGAL ON APPROPRIATE ACTION

As a rule, HR serves as a third-party, dispassionate fact finder when it comes to internal workplace investigations. Once you've completed your interviews, reviews of relevant documentation, and your investigation summary, escalate the matter to your supervisor, department head, in-house counsel, or outside employment attorney. Your job as an HR manager and investigator generally is to investigate the factual allegations and, if asked, to make a determination as to whether you believe "it is more likely than not" that the allegations occurred. You should not, however, decide whether any action violates the law or what remedial action to take against the employee. Rather, your boss, in consultation with legal counsel, should decide the impact of your factual findings and what action the organization should take.

Remember as well that practice trumps policy, meaning that your written policy may say one thing, while your practices from decisions past may have made exceptions to certain policies or allowed for differing interpretations. You won't know what your company's past practices are: only your boss and/or legal counsel will know how the firm has handled similarly situated occurrences in the past. That's another reason for you not to render judgment. Instead, once you complete your investigation, get that hot potato off your lap by passing it along to the ultimate decision-makers: your boss, department head, and possibly in-house counsel. (And don't worry—you'll get there someday when you're the "ultimate decision-maker." Chances are you'll pine for the days when you simply had to deal with the objective fact-finding piece!)

Important: Make a special note in your investigation summary of who approved the ultimate action. For example, you might write, "Sara Velasquez, SVP HR; Mindy Jones, VPHR; and Ron

McDonald, outside counsel at XYZ Law Firm, agreed that termination was warranted." Add the date and time to your notes when that decision was made.

STEP 9: TAKE APPROPRIATE ACTION

If your investigation shows that it is more likely than not that the accused employee has engaged in inappropriate behavior, the company can then decide to take appropriate corrective action. Legally speaking, corrective action generally must rectify the wrongful behavior and deter the recurrence of the inappropriate behavior in the future.

Where a violation is found, notify the accused of the findings and the specific, corrective remedial actions to be taken. The supervisor of the accused will also receive notification and should attend the disciplinary meeting in almost all circumstances. While you should share the company's conclusions with the complainant, you should not disclose details about the nature or extent of disciplinary or corrective actions to the complainant(s) and/or witness(es) unless there is a compelling reason to do so (for example, personal safety). In other words, inform the complainant that "the matter was handled and that appropriate and corrective measures were taken to ensure it doesn't happen again."

But don't state, "We issued him a final written warning for inappropriate workplace conduct and bullying." That potentially invades the individual's privacy and feeds the gossip channel. You can, however, inform the complainant of any corrective action that affects the complainant (for example, the company instructed the alleged harasser to stay away from the complainant). Encourage the complainant to report future incidents to the company that the complainant thinks are harassing or retaliatory.

In some cases, the evidence will not indicate conclusively whether the allegation(s) was founded or unfounded. If such a situation exists, the notification should state that the company has completed a thorough and timely investigation but has been unable to establish either the truth or falsity of the allegation(s).

But the company will take appropriate steps to ensure that the workers involved understand the requirements of the company's policies and appropriate law, and the company will monitor the situation to ensure compliance in the future.

STEP 10: MONITOR / FOLLOW UP TO ENSURE NO RETALIATION

Follow up with employees/complainants generally thirty and sixty days after an investigation is concluded in order to ensure that no retaliatory action has occurred. Follow up with their supervisors as well to make sure that someone "on the ground" within the group is monitoring the situation closely.

In this follow-up stage, commence an immediate investigation if there is any allegation or other evidence of retaliation.

If there is no evidence of retaliation, add a quick one-line note to your investigation file stating such in case it is later audited.

You should also be careful not to suggest that an employee who has filed a complaint is untouchable. Complainants should be protected from unlawful retaliation; they should not be shielded from legitimate adverse employment actions like progressive discipline or termination if they fail to meet an employer's legitimate performance or conduct expectations.

12

WAGE AND HOUR COMPLIANCE, REST AND MEAL PERIOD REQUIREMENTS, AND EXEMPT/ NONEXEMPT WORKER CLASSIFICATION

WAGE AND HOUR CHALLENGES REPRESENT A huge liability to your organization because noncompliance can lead to unhappy employees, government investigations, and litigation. Wage and hour liability may lurk below the surface, sometimes for years, before the problem is discovered and brought to management's attention. The problem, of course, is that once that crisis hits, companies often have very little to defend themselves unless they've been managing timekeeping procedures exceptionally well for years. If not, the long arm of the law can stretch back up to four years (depending on the state) to scrutinize paper and electronic records looking for unpaid overtime, off-the-clock work, missing meal and rest period penalties (in those periods where this is required), or other violations in wage and hour practices.

Likewise, such investigations often result in class action wage and hour lawsuits, which can be extremely time consuming and expensive to defend with hefty damage settlement demands and attorneys' fees. There are a number of quirky twists and turns in this particular area of employment law, and you can't be armed well enough in terms of protecting your organization from wage and hour liability. And while there are attorneys who make it their business suing companies for wage and hour noncompliance, the laws exist to ensure that workers are paid properly and treated fairly by their employers.

DETERMINING EXEMPTION STATUS

Exemption status will always be your first hurdle. It's your company's responsibility to pay overtime to "nonexempt" workers for hours worked in excess of forty in a week (or in some states like California, in excess of eight in a day), and it all begins with classifying your employees properly. Federal and state laws provide a limited number of exempt categories, chief among them positions in executive, administrative, professional, computer professional, and certain sales roles.

Most companies don't have any problems identifying their CEOs and vice presidents as exempt from the protections under the Fair Labor Standards Act of 1938 (FLSA), which established "overtime pay" as a penalty or tax during the Great Depression to employers for "stretching out" their existing clerical or manufacturing workforce and not adding new employees to the payroll. (Congress wanted companies to put workers back on the job at the time to climb out of the Depression, but companies stubbornly resisted, forcing employees to work excessive overtime, double shifts, and sixth and seventh days.) Employers also pretty much get that clerks, receptionists, and laborers are indeed nonexempt. In other words, they're paid for their time (rather than for their work product or results), protected by the FLSA, and docked when they come in late but paid overtime for hours worked in excess of forty in a week.

But where this gets dicey is with "wobbler" job categories like *coordinators*, *analysts*, *specialists*, and *administrators* (and, in some cases, *assistant managers*). Some companies classify these paraprofessional and junior management positions upward into the exempt category, while others place them downward into the nonexempt, overtime-eligible category. In some cases, the classification decision may withstand legal scrutiny, but just understand that if you're ever audited by the government or sued by a plaintiff's attorney, a misclassification error may lead to an award of substantial wage liability, interest, penalties, and attorney fees.

The law presumes that an employee is nonexempt (that is, entitled to overtime wages), and the burden will fall on your company to prove or otherwise demonstrate that the workers in question are indeed exempt from overtime pay. And if your company is deemed to be wrong in its classification decision, then the organization could end up with a massive back wages tab that governs the entire class of workers. The problem may be compounded by the lack of accurate time records showing how many hours the misclassified employees actually worked. Remember, all else being equal, the government liberally interprets the law to require companies to pay overtime so that workers aren't exploited or otherwise denied the additional overtime pay.

When in doubt, it's likely best to classify workers as nonexempt and pay the overtime. It could save your organization massive back wages settlements. Better yet, update your job descriptions and have qualified legal counsel review them for proper exempt versus nonexempt classification. Attorneys can't protect your organization from a judge who disagrees with your classification status for these wobbler positions, but rest assured that your attorney will err on the side of caution and likely recommend that your organization designates any questionable classifications as nonexempt to avoid the liability of a class action lawsuit.

PAYING OVERTIME CORRECTLY

In terms of paying overtime correctly, it's important to understand that overtime premiums must be paid for all overtime worked, including unapproved overtime. In fact, you're allowed to discipline an employee for working unapproved overtime, but you're not allowed to withhold the overtime pay. That would be a classic wage and hour violation. Reciprocally, in most employment settings, you have the right to instruct employees to work overtime as the workload demands. That's a basic right of any supervisor, and employees who fail to make themselves available could likewise be held to be in violation of workplace conduct standards.

Of course, before proceeding to disciplining someone formally for insubordination (that is, failure to follow a reasonable workplace directive), be sure to look at more practical issues like the reasonability of your request, the amount of notice you've given the employee, and how you would treat any and all similarly situated employees under the same circumstances. This will avoid perceptions of favoritism, bias, unfairness, and potential discrimination in the workplace. You should also be aware that when calculating the overtime rate of pay (the technical term is the *regular rate of pay*), your company may also need to include consideration of variable pay, such as shift differentials, bonuses, commissions, or other incentive pay. In some cases, an employee who receives a bonus earns a higher overtime rate rather than one who does not.

The elephant in the room when it comes to wage and hour violations is that they lend themselves to class, collective, and representative action lawsuits. In fact, plaintiffs' attorneys often question prospective nonexempt clients who come in looking for representation to pursue discrimination and wrongful termination claims to see whether they worked unpaid overtime hours or skipped lunches and breaks without pay on a frequent basis. If the answer is, "Yes, it was expected of us and happened all the time," you could very well see a class action wage and hour claim attached to your ex-employee's other legal charges. And costs add up quickly. Calculations typically go back several years, and it's not uncommon for damages resulting from unpaid overtime plus attorneys' fees to settle in the six- to seven-figure range, depending on the size of your company and the number of workers in the class.

The lesson here? Don't panic if one of your nonexempt employees misses a break or lunch period on occasion. But don't become known as a company where skipped meals and breaks become the norm or where working unpaid overtime occurs on an "expected" basis. If you steer clear of developing that type of reputation by respecting the law and treating your nonexempt workers fairly, then occasional, nonsytemic lapses probably won't pose much of a serious legal risk.

AVOIDING "LUNCH AT THE DESK" SYNDROME

That being said, you should encourage your nonexempt team members to get away from the office (or at least their desk) during lunch and rest periods. If taking lunch at the desk becomes the norm or expectation, it will be assumed that your hourly staffers were expected to pick up the phone if it rang, keep an eye on email, or attend to other matters of business. And that, unfortunately, violates the definition of a true rest or meal period (in those states where it is required). If an employee performs *any* work during an off-the-clock meal break, this may give rise to a claim for off-the-clock work. Moreover, in some cases, courts have held that meal breaks shortened too much by work should not have been off the clock at all; in other words, the entire meal period was invalidated.

Oh, and if you and your employees don't have a record of all the times they skipped their breaks and meal periods, then the courts or the Department of Labor will gladly share their calculation tools and tell you how much your company owes in back wages and attorneys' fees based on their estimates. Just remember that for nonexempt, hourly employees, breaks and lunches are for breaks and lunches—not for work. There's no need to surprise your organization with a class action wage and hour lawsuit because you failed to adhere to the law in this very fundamental respect.

There are other rules, of course. Are meal or rest period premiums payable for missed lunches or breaks? How many rest and meal periods are required under ten- or twelve-hour shifts? Does an employee need to work a minimum number of hours before rest or meal periods come into play? What if you suspect that an employee is working off the clock in a remote work setting? Whatever the scenario, rest assured that plaintiffs' attorneys have seen them all and may be ready to pounce as soon as the opportunity presents itself. It's in your and your company's best interests to make sure that you are familiar with the rules and constantly on the lookout for exceptions. If you haven't been trained in this critical area, ask your employer to set up a wage and hour training workshop so that everyone on the management team is on the same page. Then train your nonexempt staff members so that everyone's on the same page regarding the company's policies, practices, and expectations.

13

HR DEPARTMENT OF ONE
HR in Start-Ups and Small Firms

WHEN SMALLER ORGANIZATIONS OPT TO CREATE their first HR departments, it's not uncommon to promote someone into their first HR management position. Likewise, external market recruitment may be the way to hire someone with previous solo HR experience. Whatever the result, serving smaller companies as an "HR department of one" is no easy task. Every topic in this book—and many others—will contribute to your success, and it's important that you keep things simple and establish core rules and goals that you measure, track, and manage. Rest assured, the daily challenges of HR administration and "people problems" will likely keep you busy enough. Establishing a foundational HR practice, despite all the interruptions and changes in plan that are common to the solo HR discipline, is the goal of this chapter. It will help you keep your eye on the bigger picture and establish your employment brand as an HR expert in your "department of one."

YOUR CORE PRIORITIES

Key focus areas will vary based on the company and industry you're in. Still, the elements that follow should help you in most cases, although swapping out one or two of the suggested elements below is expected. The key to establishing your solo HR department's foundational principles lies in finding balance among your various priorities—bringing the full range of HR expertise to your organization, balancing competing priorities, and working collaboratively with your non-HR counterparts. Let's partner together to identify best practices and maximize your and your HR department's success in smaller organizations.

Whether you're launching your company's first HR department or inheriting an existing HR function when you join the firm, the following considerations may be an excellent place to start.

MACRO GOALS

1. Develop your overall HR plan and document your HR strategy (in collaboration with your boss, of course).
2. Set up a plan for regulatory compliance (that is, areas where formal government reporting is required or where penalties and fines may come into play if your organization is unprepared).
3. Determine competitive recruiting and onboarding practices and procedures.
4. Build a strategy for effective compensation and benefits.
5. Master HR technology to boost efficiency and compliance.
6. Draft an employee handbook as well as a policies and procedures manual to enhance communication and guide your employee relations practice.
7. Create a culture of trust, inclusion, and respect by practicing MBWA (Management by Walking Around) and modeling the behaviors that you wish to bring out in others.

Each of these core areas can be developed more deeply, of course. For example, to point three above on recruiting and onboarding, you can easily add "building a comprehensive talent strategy" that includes internal talent and leadership development, succession planning and performance management. Small companies and start-ups that are ready to hire their first HR manager are typically projecting rapid growth. As such, a strategic plan and forecast that includes both external talent sourcing and internal talent development makes for a much deeper dive into this broader category of "recruitment."

If you agree with these seven basic foundational elements, then use them to guide your HR practice. In other words, the majority of what you work on should fall into one of these seven areas, especially in your first year as a newly minted or recently hired manager. This makes for a wise strategy and goal-setting exercise. Be sure to tie your HR strategy to the organization's vision, mission, and values as specifically as possible. Breaking each one of these seven broader goals into bite-size pieces will make things easier and more manageable for you. For example, the following tasks—which are broad projects in and of themselves—may help you reach and exceed the macro goals established above.

DEVELOPING YOUR HR PLAN

What should your HR strategic plan look like? What should it include? And most important, how should you construct it? First, understand that this exercise should be a team sport. Work closely with your immediate superior to map out your initial thoughts. If your boss isn't the CEO or business owner, then be sure that this escalates to that individual's level before it's finalized. Once it's complete or near to being completed, you and your boss might want to share it with other members of the senior leadership team to both (a) elicit additional feedback and (b) inform and align senior management about what your role will focus on. A sample HR Plan or strategy statement might look like this:

> XYZ Company's HR Strategic Plan focuses on attracting, developing, and retaining the most qualified talent to accommodate our future growth plans. Its purpose is to establish expectations regarding leadership, communication, and team building, meet regulatory compliance requirements, and create a friendly and inclusive

work environment where employees can do their very best work every day with peace of mind.

To that end, the HR Plan will endeavor to achieve the following objectives:

- Attract, retain, and develop top talent
- Ensure compliance with employment laws and regulations
- Foster a positive and inclusive work environment
- Administer traditional HR functions, including recruitment, compensation, benefits, employee relations, training and development, and leave of absence management
- Enhance employee engagement and performance

This HR Strategic Plan is considered a living, breathing document, where objectives and priorities may change from time to time. It is intended to capture the spirit of the human resources department and its priorities and contributions to XYZ's growth and development through its workforce.

Feel free to use this as a starting point or begin anew. But once your focus is established and shared, it helps align your department's function with everyone else's, and that's an optimal way to start. What gets measured gets managed, and pronouncing your objectives and goals formally makes for a clean and transparent exercise where you control the message, your boss and/or CEO / business owner contributes to it, and you establish appropriate expectations for your key clients and stakeholders. (It also makes it easier to say no to certain "oddball" requests that fall outside the scope of your strategic plan.)

Further, for your own records (and to be shared with your boss), the following section explains how to break down each of your priorities using the core focal areas suggested here.

ADDRESSING REGULATORY COMPLIANCE

Partner with your CEO, COO, and/or director of finance or risk management to determine which reporting requirements govern your firm. Mark all deliverables down in chronological order on a shared calendar so that you know—month by month—what's coming due and what hard deadlines await. Share that finished timeline with those same parties so they're aware of what you're responsible for and can likewise support you with collateral documentation from their areas that you'll need to report on. Important: before submitting any formal reports to a government entity, ensure that you've gained the necessary internal approvals from anyone on this shortlist—CEO / business owner, VP of legal affairs, chief financial officer, and/or director of safety and facilities.

HR checklists are critically important to all HR practices but especially in smaller organizations. Creating a checklist makes your HR practice "dummy-proof," for lack of a better term, because few details will fall through the cracks. And without anyone on your own team to partner with, you'll want to make sure that your submissions are spotless and fully vetted by the stakeholder team listed above. Consider creating checklists for any of the following practices:

- ❏ New Hire Checklist
- ❏ Employee Onboarding Checklist (including computer and cell phone advance setup)
- ❏ Employment Recordkeeping and Personnel File Checklist (including a master list for your immediate supervisor about where files are stored, including personnel files, medical record files, I-9s, and the like)
- ❏ Timekeeping Practices Checklist (including rest and meal period compliance, overtime calculations, leave time, travel time, and remote work timekeeping)
- ❏ Emergency Preparedness Checklist (including disaster planning and recovery)

❏ Employee Offboarding Checklist (including termination preparation procedures like final checks, COBRA, and unemployment insurance pamphlet distribution)

Other checklists may include I-9 Audits and, depending on your organization's size, Affirmative Action, EEO-1 Reporting, and the like. The point is that you won't need to create all your own documents, templates, policies, and checklists. As an HR department of one, it's worth investing in an HR subscription resource or information platform, especially when working in challenging states like California, New York, New Jersey, Massachusetts, or Illinois, where it's critical to have real-time access to legal updates and compliance, policies, and forms.

Finally, an HR audit may be appropriate to capture the organization's current practices in key people areas. This makes for an excellent quarterly goal. HR audits typically aim to

- determine the current state of your organization's HR practices, policies, and procedures;
- determine what serious risks, if any, threaten your organization in terms of legal compliance or personnel challenges; and
- establish a plan to address those gaps within a particular deliverable time period.

HR audits provide a deeper-dive analysis in terms of personnel file compliance (that is, secure, separate files for I-9 and medical records), wage and hour compliance, employee privacy rights, HR/people analytics and metrics, diversity review, HR budgets and spending, bonus/incentive/commission plans, OSHA inspection results, and handbook and policy receipt signatures from all employees. Templates are available online or from the Society for Human Resource Management (SHRM), and vendors are available to conduct HR audit due diligence for you, usually at a reasonable cost.

INITIATING COMPETITIVE RECRUITMENT
AND ONBOARDING PRACTICES

Expect your first client visits to come from concerned hiring managers who haven't been able to fill open positions for extended periods of time. What ideas do you have? Do you have any external relationships with vendors that can help us? What will be particularly effective for us and still keep our expenses in check? Ah, nothing like a bit of panic to welcome you into a new role or company and get your "baptism by fire" underway! While it's quite logical that you'll be dragged into the fray (or strategically invited to problem-solve), you'll want to take a quick snapshot of your recruitment and termination metrics first so that you have an appropriate handle on the bigger picture of trends and patterns in talent acquisition, retention, and loss. Look first to answer these questions to gain an upper hand on the challenges you'll soon face:

- What is your current employee count?
- What percentage of your workforce is full-time, part-time (benefit eligible), part-time (nonbenefit eligible), per diem, temporary, and the like?
- What percentage of your workforce is exempt versus nonexempt?
- What is the average tenure of your current workforce?
- What is your average employee pay (consider excluding the CEO/owner or other C-level executives whose pay may be significantly higher than everyone else's and therefore throw off your calculations)?
- What is the average age of your current workforce?
- How does your workforce break down in terms of male versus female and over forty versus under forty?
- How many hires were made in the previous twelve months? How many hires were made per quarter over that same

time period? (When do hiring spikes appear to occur?)

- Internal mobility: How many positions were filled internally versus externally? For internally filled positions, what percentage were lateral moves versus promotions?
- What is your annual turnover percentage? What percentage of turnover is voluntary (resignation) versus involuntary (termination or layoff)?
- What is your average time to start (that is, the time gap from when a job is posted to when a new hire begins)? Distinguish between exempt and nonexempt populations.
- What sources provide you with the most hires and the greatest return on your recruitment advertising investment (for example, LinkedIn, Indeed, or other job boards)? Does your organization recruit on boutique diversity websites to increase the size of and simultaneously diversify your talent pool?
- Do you have an internal referral program and, if not, would one be worth considering? Likewise, do you have a "buddy system" for onboarding new hires through the first ninety days?
- What new community relationships may be available to increase the applicant flow (including tech schools, junior colleges, internship programs, and the like)?

Why is it ideal to have all these details, some of which sound personal and nonbusiness related (for example, age, gender, and the like)? Because you're looking to determine your *story*. HR is in many ways about storytelling, but nowhere more so than when it comes to describing your workforce. For example, a "workforce story" might sound like this:

> Our average tenure is 4.3 years, and relative to our industry, we're doing a great job retaining talent. Likewise, our turnover hovers around 10 percent a year, year in and year out, which is ideal, so we're not losing people unnecessarily to the competition. That

being said, our average employee age is sixty-two, so we have to consider hiring new talent to replace those who will likely retire in the next few years. Also, we're 70 percent male, and we realize that building our talent pipeline to capture more women is important. We likewise want to focus on trimming our hiring time, which currently takes eleven weeks on average and isn't competitive with the market. Overall, we're overly reliant on internal referrals (often family members of existing employees) and want to identify new sources of fresh talent, both by expanding our use of custom job boards that attract diverse and disabled workers and by building relationships with the local junior college to participate in their career-day job fairs and possibly launch an internship program.

You get the idea. Every story will change over time, but what's critical is that you can tell yours. And you'll only be able to do that if you're relying on objective metrics that capture the broader sense of who your workforce is. With those parameters in mind, you can then begin to recruit one-off open positions within your organization. (And your boss will love the data!) Understand as well that this ties in effectively to strategic staffing initiatives, which involve a well-thought-out forecast based on projected sales growth, market conditions, the ability to onboard at a reasonable pace, and managing head count as well as salary costs. These topics should be top of mind for HR departments of one.

DRAFTING AN EMPLOYEE HANDBOOK TO ENHANCE COMMUNICATION AND GUIDE YOUR EMPLOYEE RELATIONS PRACTICE

Likewise, a common task you'll be charged with as a new HR manager in a small to medium-sized company lies in creating the organization's first employee handbook. In fact, it's often the first thing that the CEO / business owner will ask for. It's a noble ask for a reason: by the time an organization is ready to hire its first

HR manager, there's likely been a lot of one-off exceptions to various rules made. Hiring you represents order, structure, and an approval process that the CEO / business owner has likely been wanting to put in place for quite some time. Their logic is simple: if the rules and guidelines are written down, it will become much easier for everyone to "follow the rules." Does that make sense? Sure. Does it always work that way? Not necessarily! The old adage "rules are meant to be broken" is still alive and well in corporate America, and simply mapping out every rule and guideline cleanly on a piece of paper won't solve all your organizational problems. But it's a very healthy start and in fact the only place to start if greater consistency is your CEO's end goal.

Creating written expectations that outline the steps that managers or employees are expected to take makes things administratively much more doable. Efficiency and alignment will truly make a difference for those who enjoy following rules and feeling more confident in the "letter of the law" to guide their thinking and recommendations. On the other hand, those who break the proverbial rules will end up in your office and drive your employee-relations practice, where you (and your boss and/or in-house or outside counsel) determine whether progressive discipline or outright termination may be warranted for particular egregious offenses. Having your rules and policies written down goes a long way in ensuring fairness and equity in your handling of tough situations. Written guidelines can likewise come in exceptionally handy when you're challenged by a plaintiff's attorney for wrongful termination, discrimination, harassment, and the like. So, look to this exercise as a critical imperative for your boss—and one that will affect your organization's culture moving forward.

Important: When it comes to creating employee handbooks, enlist the services of a qualified employment defense attorney in more challenging states like California, New York, New Jersey, Massachusetts, and Illinois. Attorneys routinely create handbooks for companies. And the laws that govern the workplace can be tricky and filled with exceptions. My recommendation, therefore, is to work with qualified legal counsel when drafting such documents rather than outsourcing the exercise to less expensive and less qualified lay consultants. That attorney moniker on your work will pay for itself quickly should you ever have to defend your policies before a court of law.

That insulation from liability is an additional but critical benefit to justify the creation of your handbook in the first place. Of course, if you're in a more "employer-friendly" state with lesser complexity in the HR and employment law space, a handbook builder from either an HRIS or other established vendor may make most sense. In such cases, you can build the handbook yourself (which can save a lot of money), vet it internally with your CEO, COO, and in-house attorney, and then send the finished product to qualified outside counsel for final review. In all cases, however, I recommend that qualified employment law counsel blesses your handbook before you release it.

CREATING A CULTURE OF TRUST, INCLUSION, AND RESPECT

I didn't save this entry for last because it's the least important aspect or element of your new role. In fact, it's quite the opposite: it's the summation of your entire contribution to the organization. When an organization makes its first HR hire, the individual's soft skills are essential qualities that are focused on. Does the individual communicate effectively? Can they lead and influence others in a positive and constructive way? Are they strong team builders, people who can bring normally conflictive teams or departments together to find common ground and collaborate on larger projects to attain strong outcomes? Do they possess the natural empathy and emotional intelligence to help others who may be in need, either for personal or workplace-related reasons? These are the key drivers of your and every HR manager's success. The greatest part about a solo HR practice is that you get to handle everything directly. You know your people intimately, you serve as the liaison to senior executive leadership, and you have the ability to set sail in a strategic direction all your own. Just make sure you've got your strategy and priorities down pat so you don't feel overwhelmed or fail to see the forest for the trees.

14

PREPARING FOR SURVEYORS AND GOVERNMENT AUDITORS
Your Essential Checklists

NO MATTER WHAT INDUSTRY YOU WORK IN, government audits pose significant challenges to most HR organizations. We've all seen the headlines—I-9, OSHA, wage and hour, immigration, and other audits can result in significant fines and penalties. Much will depend on your company's industry, size, and specific HR-related practices, but make no mistake: you won't want your company to incur large fines and liabilities under your watch. As such, a keen eye is required to ensure (a) that your department is ready for a surprise audit at any time and (b) everyone on the team knows where the key materials (cabinets, shared drives, files, binders, and the like) are located should you not be on-site at the time of the auditor's visit.

Like other topics in this book, the area of audits and audit preparation is vast. The simplest way to walk through this together is by reviewing sample checklists that will help you on a practical basis. Oh, and please don't look down on checklists as simplistic or demeaning tools: airline pilots use checklists before every flight, brain surgeons use checklists prior to complicated surgeries, and quality control professionals use checklists to achieve consistently improved outcomes. Atul Gawande wrote a famous book called *The Checklist Manifesto* where he admits that using checklists can feel demeaning to professionals. Yet overseeing tasks or projects and ensuring nothing important is forgotten during execution is critically important as you prepare your internal audits and identify gaps or weaknesses that you'll want to address before a government auditor shows up on your doorstep. Let's walk through this together.

STEP 1: DETERMINE WHICH LAWS APPLY TO YOU

Based on your employee count and the state you're in, whether you're a government contractor, and the like, different thresholds apply regarding the laws and guidelines covering some of the following areas:

Affirmative Action	Illiteracy Accommodation	Prior Salary History Ban
Alcohol and Drug Rehabilitation	Immigration Reform and Control Act (IRCA)	Privacy
Americans with Disabilities Act	Injury and Illness Prevention Program (IIPP)	School and Childcare Activities
Ban the Box	Independent Contractors	School Appearance Leave
Child Labor	Jury Day Time Off	Smoking in the Workplace
Civil Air Patrol	Lactation Accommodation	Unemployment Insurance
Crime Victims' Leave	Mandatory Sexual Harassment Training	Training Leave for Emergency Rescue Personnel
COBRA	Military Leave (USERRA)	Volunteer Civil Service Leave
Disability Insurance	Military Spouse Leave	Worker Adjustment and Retraining Notification—WARN Act (plant closings)

Discrimination Laws (federal)	New Employee Reporting	Workers' Compensation (fill in)
Discrimination Laws (state)	Organ and Bone Marrow Donor's Leave	Other 1:
Domestic Violence, Sexual Assault, and Stalking Victims' Leave (legal proceedings / reasonable accommodation / medical treatment)	Paid Family Leave	Other 2:
Employee Safety	Paid Sick Leave	Other 3:
Equal Employment Opportunity (EEO) Reporting	Posters and Notices	Other 4:
Family Medical Leave Act / FMLA (and state equivalent)	Pregnancy Disability Laws	Other 5:

It likewise becomes necessary to determine who is an employee. The definition of who is counted as an employee may vary depending on the legal requirements at issue. For some laws, you must include temporary employees and independent contractors to determine your employee count. When in doubt, check with qualified legal counsel to ensure your focus is correct as you prepare your audit analysis.

STEP 2: DEVELOPING APPROPRIATE CHECKLISTS FOR KEY EXPOSURES

Portions of the following checklists incorporate elements recommended by the Society for Human Resource Management (SHRM) and are reprinted with SHRM's permission. Again, the samples below are only partial checklists. The full checklists as well as other checklists are available to SHRM members on the SHRM website at www.shrm.org.

HR GENERAL COMPLIANCE AUDIT CHECKLISTS

FAIR LABOR STANDARDS ACT (FLSA)

- ❏ Wage and hour claims pending, settled, or threatened
- ❏ Wage/Hour Division investigations
- ❏ Conciliation agreements with the Department of Labor

OFFICE OF FEDERAL CONTRACTOR COMPLIANCE PROGRAMS (OFCCP)

- ❏ Affirmative action programs
- ❏ Conciliation agreements
- ❏ Charges or complaints alleging violation of Executive Order 11246, Section 503, or VEVRAA requirements
- ❏ Files and correspondence regarding prior OFCCP audits or investigations

EQUAL EMPLOYMENT OPPORTUNITY COMMISSION (EEOC)

- ❏ Prior charges
- ❏ Potential charges
- ❏ Pending charges
- ❏ Litigation arising from charges

OCCUPATIONAL SAFETY AND HEALTH ACT

- ❏ Complaints
- ❏ Investigation files
- ❏ Citations

NATIONAL LABOR RELATIONS BOARD

- ❏ Collective bargaining agreements
- ❏ Existing petitions
- ❏ Files concerning prior petitions
- ❏ Existing unfair labor practice charges
- ❏ Files concerning prior unfair labor practice charges
- ❏ Litigation with the National Labor Relations Board

PENSION BENEFIT GUARANTEE CORPORATION
- ❏ Correspondence
- ❏ Inquiries
- ❏ Charges and litigation

OTHER LITIGATION
- ❏ Whistleblower claims
- ❏ Wrongful discharge matters
- ❏ Breach of contract claims
- ❏ Any and all federal, state, municipal and administrative decrees, judgments, decisions, opinions, or settlement agreements issued or entered into either for or against the company in employment matters
- ❏ Any present or ongoing employment litigation brought by past or present employees or on behalf of past or present employees by any agency of the federal, state, or municipal government
- ❏ Schedule of any employment-related legal proceedings or charges during the past five years with settlement costs, if any
- ❏ Any litigation not otherwise disclosed concerning employment matters

REPORTING COMPLIANCE
- ❏ Copies of EEO-1 reports for past five years
- ❏ Copies of VETS-4212 reports for past five years
- ❏ Copy of affirmative action plan
- ❏ OSHA reports 300, 300A, and 301 for the past five years
- ❏ PPACA annual reporting (Patient Protections and Affordable Care Act)

EEO-1 REPORTING CHECKLIST
- ❏ Determine if your company is required to complete the EEO-1 Report.

All private employers with one hundred or more employees

and

All federal contractors and first-tier subcontractors with fifty or more employees *and* contracts of at least $50,000 are obligated to complete and file the report each year.

❏ Determine which form(s) must be completed:

Single-establishment companies: Standard 100 Form

Multiestablishment companies:

1. Consolidated Report (Type 2): a report including all employees of the company categorized by race/ethnicity, sex, and job category
2. Headquarters Report (Type 3): a report covering those working at the headquarters office, including those working from home
3. Establishment Report (Type 4): a separate report for each branch with fifty or more employees
4. Establishment Report (Type 8): a consolidated report with all employees who work at branches with fewer than fifty employees

❏ Select one (1) pay period within the fourth quarter (October, November, or December) of the current survey year to complete the EEO-1 Report. The current survey year is the year prior to the year the EEO-1 is submitted.
❏ Ensure that self-identification forms and data are available from each employee during the pay period selected. Organize employee data by listing all employees by location, job category, and then by ethnicity, race, and gender.
❏ Complete the EEO-1 Report online on or before March 31 following the survey year (unless a delay is announced).

❑ Start the filing process by completing the EEO-1 Online Application. First-time filers will need to register prior to completing the EEO-1 Report.

❑ Follow the prompts to enter employment data into the online form. If an employer has challenges entering the data, contact the EEOC Filer Support Team.

❑ Retain records for at least one year from the date of the making of the record.

EMPLOYMENT RECORDKEEPING CHECKLIST

Employee Files

❑ Are files maintained in a locked and secure cabinet, or have proper electronic security features been developed?

❑ Have all documents that contain sensitive/confidential information such as Social Security numbers been removed from the personnel file?

❑ Are personnel files organized in a logical manner so that information is easy to find?

❑ Is there a policy regarding employee access to personnel files in compliance with state law?

❑ Are individual files audited internally for compliance on a regular schedule?

Medical Files

❑ Are records containing employee medical information kept separate from employee personnel files?

❑ Is employee medical information securely stored with limited access?

I-9 Forms

❑ Are I-9 forms and relevant documentation kept separate from employee personnel files?

❑ Are I-9 forms securely stored with limited access?

❏ Are I-9 forms audited internally on an established schedule?

EEO Records

❏ Are equal employment opportunity (EEO) data records maintained separately from personnel files and used only for reporting purposes such as for an affirmative action program (AAP), EEO-1 reporting, and internal diversity tracking?

❏ Are EEO records securely stored with limited access?

Terminated Employee Files

❏ Are terminated files securely stored with limited access?

❏ Is there a regular (monthly or quarterly) disposal plan for documents that have exceeded record retention requirements?

❏ Are records that have met or exceeded record retention requirements disposed of via shredding or fully destroying these records prior to disposal?

❏ Are files related to a current or potential lawsuit maintained by legal counsel or otherwise marked to be exempted from any disposal process until after the suit is closed?

❏ Is there a written record retention and destruction policy and procedure?

I-9 AUDIT CHECKLIST

ITEMS NEEDED FOR AUDIT

❏ List of current employees hired since November 6, 1986

❏ List of employees terminated in the past three years

❏ Original or electronic copies of all I-9 forms (both current employee forms as well as forms for terminated employees within current retention requirements)

- ❏ *Handbook for Employers M-274* published by the USCIS (optional)
- ❏ Current version of Form I-9
- ❏ Audit Log
- ❏ I-9 Audit How-to Guide

REVIEW I-9 FORMS BY SECTION

Section 1

- ❏ Name (including other last names used, past or present), address, and date of birth are completed.
- ❏ Social Security number is entered if employer participates in the E-Verify program.
- ❏ Appropriate citizen/immigration status box is checked.
- ❏ Lawful permanent residents have provided their seven- to nine-digit Alien Registration Number (A-Number) or USCIS Number.
- ❏ Aliens have provided an Alien Registration Number / USCIS Number or Form I-94 Admission Number or Foreign Passport Number.
- ❏ Employee signed and dated the form no later than the first day of employment.
- ❏ Preparer or translator section is completed if someone other than the employee completed Section 1 on behalf of the employee.

Section 2

- ❏ Employee's name is entered as it appears in section 1.
- ❏ The number is entered that correlates with the citizenship or immigration status box the employee selected in section 1.
- ❏ One document from list A is listed and completed, or a combination of one document *each* from list B and list C are listed and completed.

❏ Documents have been entered into the correct section (for example, list B item is, in fact, listed under list B and not list C or list A).

❏ If photocopies of documents are kept, copies of documents are maintained for all employees.

❏ The employee's first day of employment is entered.

❏ All information in the certification section has been entered and a representative of the company has signed and printed his or her name and dated the form within three days of the employee's first day of employment.

❏ The business name and full address are entered.

Section 3

❏ Section 3 is completed if the employee's work authorization expired or if the employee was rehired within three years from the date the I-9 form was previously completed.

❏ If the employee's name changed, the new name is entered in block A.

CORRECT ERRORS

Missing I-9 Forms

❏ Have the employee complete section 1 of the current version of the I-9 form immediately.

❏ Inspect the employee's original documents and complete section 2.

❏ Use current dates; do not backdate the form except that the employee's original hire date should be entered in section 2.

❏ Do not continue to employ individuals who are unable to provide acceptable documents as required.

❏ Do not re-create the I-9 form without the employee's presence or without examining the employee's original documents.

❏ Do not re-create the I-9 form for terminated employees; rather, complete a note to file with an explanation.

TIMEKEEPING PRACTICES CHECKLIST

❏ Implement a method of timekeeping such as a time clock, paper time card, or electronic system.

❏ Define the workweek (any seven consecutive twenty-four-hour periods).

❏ Establish procedures in accordance with the payroll schedule for submitting timekeeping records for approval and processing.

❏ Establish a policy requiring employees to record all hours worked, including:

❏ start and end times each day
❏ rest and meal periods as required by state law
❏ on-call hours worked
❏ leave time (holiday, personal, vacation, and so on)
❏ travel time that occurs during their workday
❏ travel time when traveling away from home or overnight
❏ attendance at training programs and meetings

❏ Define the process for making corrections to time records, including any approval required.

❏ Maintain time records in compliance with federal and state laws.

❏ Store time records securely and protected from damage (for example, floods, fire).

❏ Limit access to time records to those with a legitimate business purpose.

A SMART TIP

These audits make for a great exercise for all staff members because they help them feel more confident and informed by providing broader exposure to the entire HR organization as a whole. Inviting team members to take the lead in particular audit areas is likewise a great stretch assignment because it puts emerging leaders in control of real-time challenges that require concrete solutions. It also designates them as subject matter experts in that space. What an excellent opportunity to set quarterly individual goals and capture annual team accomplishments!

PART THREE

STRATEGIC HR AND THE FUTURE OF THE HR PROFESSION

OPENING ADVICE

BEFORE JUMPING INTO PART THREE, it's important to emphasize that as a manager, especially a new manager, your access to executive-level information and decision-making is somewhat limited. Depending on the size of your organization, the same goes for directors, vice presidents, and even senior vice presidents. (Yes, until you get to the chief human resources officer or executive vice president level where you're reporting directly to the C-suite, you likely won't have the full picture surrounding decisions that are made or key programs that are rolled out.) As a result, a more effective approach for you is to be patient, support your organization's initiatives, and look for ways to volunteer and add value to whatever new programs, policies, or challenges come your way from the C-suite.

Too many new managers jump to conclusions, voice frustration over their organizations' decisions or actions, and come across as sources of negativity, disloyalty, or disruption. While speaking out at times is critical to your professional and career development as well as your sense of ethics, it always makes sense to initially assume that you don't have all the facts that led to a particular decision. Hence, the optimal approach is for you to assume good intentions through analysis and solid decision-making, unless proven otherwise. And when in doubt, err on the side of being a managerial team player. Critical business decisions are never easy, and sometimes senior leaders have to make calls that are the lesser of two evils, may appear to be driven more by legal compliance than the greatest benefit to your workforce, or may simply focus on cost control. Until you're sitting in that seat, you simply won't have all the facts, background considerations, or pressures that are associated with senior-level executive leadership and decision-making. After all, when you attain your seat in the C-suite, the last thing you'll want is a newly minted manager calling all your decisions into question.

Therefore, be supportive. Be patient and understanding. Recognize that, generally speaking, the key decision-makers do not approach their roles and responsibilities casually. Rather, they engage deeply and carefully in their areas and do their best under the circumstances and given the challenges they face. I'm not saying, "Go along to get along," but I am saying that without all the key facts—many of which often cannot be shared due to the confidential nature of the business considerations behind the scenes—it helps to have supportive managers throughout your department who understand the process and give you the benefit of the doubt. Play your part as a representative of your department and make yourself part of the solution. The days of "I don't agree with this, but they're making us do it" should end once you join the management ranks. You *are* the company and its decisions. It's important that you support its priorities and make them your own to the extent possible.

15

STRATEGIC HR AND EARNING YOUR PROVERBIAL "SEAT AT THE TABLE"

SO MUCH IS SAID ABOUT "STRATEGIC HR" and "earning your seat at the table of senior leadership" that it's a topic well worth addressing as you launch your HR management career path. The first question, therefore, is what is *strategic HR leadership*? If you run a simple Google search on that term, you'll find entries that read:

- Leverage HR to execute business strategy.
- Recognize how value is created through HR.
- Draw on frameworks for driving growth and change via HR management.
- Understand and model approaches for making decisions under risk and uncertainty.
- Ensure that policies, culture, and working practices enable high performance and organizational capability.
- Address and solve business problems and directly contribute to major long-term business objectives.
- Provide a framework linking people management and development practices to long-term business goals and outcomes.

Likewise, if you research "steps and activities necessary for strategic HR management," you'll likely find:

- Assess your current workforce.
- Create employee development plans.
- Perform a gap analysis.
- Create a succession plan.
- Decide how to increase resources for the future.

In fact, there are "stages," "steps," "pillars," "tools," "elements," and many other pieces of advice on how to become a strategic HR player and earn your seat at the table, including:

- scheduling time to think strategically;
- understanding the needs and challenges of your company;
- gathering data and understanding metrics;
- developing and implementing plans; and
- forecasting into the future.

I don't know about you, but this all sounds fairly theoretical and wishy-washy to me. With so many priorities and emergencies facing us day in and day out, what should we really be focusing on to develop our strategic HR thinking skills? I'm glad you asked . . . There are certain steps that you can initiate and/or certainly volunteer to become a part of as a first-time HR manager. In terms of the big picture, these steps are premised on sharing your ideas with your manager, keeping the financial and budgeting impact in mind, and making the concept of "creating a strategic mindset" a central part of your personal career development toolbox. There are four powerful HR steps that you can start implementing on day one to help take your career, your team, and your organization to the next level.

STEP ONE: GET THE BIG PICTURE BY LEVERAGING HUMAN CAPITAL DATA (A.K.A. WORKFORCE METRICS)

In today's business world, nothing is more important than solid data. It helps improve efficiency and productivity and allows leaders to make faster, more effective decisions to improve outcomes. Human capital data is gathered from your employees and provides a wealth of information about the entire employee experience. It can help organizations stop playing guessing games and make concrete connections between employee behavior and strategic action planning.

Another meaningful benefit of collecting and analyzing human capital data is to help your workforce strengthen and upgrade their existing skills and acquire new skills they may need in order to move forward. This is done by analyzing the competencies of individuals within your organization and identifying potential skill gaps that may limit future organizational flexibility and the potential to withstand change and grow. This process will also help better track employees seeking development while simultaneously helping managers and leaders craft career paths for their advancement. (These are likewise core elements of talent management and talent development.)

To truly capitalize on the myriad measurable benefits associated with human capital data, consider researching the following organization-wide metrics, which can then be broken down into divisional or departmental subcategories:

Average Employee Tenure	Internal Transfer Rate
Average Employee Compensation	Internal Promotion Rate
Full-Time versus Part-Time versus "Other" Status	Average Employee Age + Percentage Over/Under 40
Percentage On-Site versus Remote	Male versus Female Breakdown
Average Performance Appraisal Scores—Last Three Years	Diversity Breakdown

Primary versus Secondary Reasons for Progressive Disciplinary Actions (Numbers)	Breakdown by Education, Licensure, or Certification
Primary versus Secondary Reasons for Leaving the Organization (through Exit Interview Surveys)	# Cross-Trained, # High Potential, # "Ready for Promotion Now" Employees (Succession Planning)
Turnover Rate: Voluntary versus Involuntary	Trends in Employee Feedback (via Climate Surveys or Focus Groups)

Your goal in conducting these analyses lies in identifying the organizational context that influences the HR strategy. People are your organization's primary profit lever. Do you (and, more importantly, does your senior leadership team) understand the drivers, trends, and patterns that make your workforce unique?

Let's look at some examples:

- If the average performance review score of your entire organization is "5—Exceeds Expectations," what may be missing from your frontline operational leaders' talent discernment capabilities? (Everyone can't be perfect, after all!)
- If certain operational areas have a less diverse workforce, what can be done to increase recruiting and retention?
- If people cite "Failure to get along with my supervisor" as the number one reason why they leave the organization, what kind of management training interventions can be initiated to strengthen leadership muscle and turn that problem around?
- What are you doing differently to engage fully remote or hybrid workers who may be feeling lonely, isolated, or out of connection with the "mother ship"?
- If your employee population at a particular location skews younger or shorter tenured, what kinds of solutions can you recommend to stem turnover?

- If you have multiple generations in one location—for example, the five generations of Traditionalists, baby boomers, Gen X, Gen Y, and Gen Z—what can you do to foster a greater sense of partnership, camaraderie, and collaboration?
- If you suspect that your average pay is low relative to the external market, what kind of budget approval can you obtain to create a salary plan and bring wages up to market within a reasonable period of time (typically six to eighteen months)?
- If your internal pay structure has inequities and disparities, such as employees with the same job title and similar responsibilities being paid significantly different salaries or even subjected to different job classifications, can you design and obtain budgetary approval for a new structure that removes the inequities and misclassifications within a reasonable time period (typically six to eighteen months)?
- And most important, where does your internal promotion rate tend to choke off? In other words, at what level do internal promotions no longer work (for example, at the manager, director, or VP level) to fill open positions, and what can be done to grow internal talent to get past that choke point?

Here's how some strategic HR thinking worked at one blood plasma collection organization that was suffering from low procurement volume. The donor center managers claimed that donors needed to be paid more to entice them to donate plasma (which can be donated twice per week). The HR team proffered an alternative solution: look to the human capital metrics to determine what differentiates top donor centers from mediocre or low-volume producers. A scorecard was developed that used only one operational metric—monthly donor volume—that served as the benchmark for all centers. Then human capital metrics were added:

- average tenure, age, diversity demographics
- time to fill open positions
- voluntary versus involuntary turnover numbers and percentages
- number of triple cross-trained employees (donor processors, plasma processors, and phlebotomists)
- number of employees who transitioned from plasma production to quality control
- number of high-potential employees
- average performance review score of all employees at each location
- number of progressive disciplinary interventions; top reasons for discipline

It didn't take long for the glaring differences among donor centers to come to light. Some had exceptionally high turnover, some particularly low production. Those became the centers of focus, and in a number of cases, similar trends and patterns emerged among them: 120 days to fill open positions (compared to an average of forty days for the company as a whole); few cross-trained employees and no high-potential employees ready to promote; excessive disciplinary actions (that is, writing up everyone for every mistake) versus writing up no one (despite low production volume); high average performance review scores despite low donor center production levels, along with similar types of findings across the array of workforce metrics.

The glaring differences associated with human capital data were directly parallel to the glaring differences in the overall performance of the various donor centers. These differentials highlighted the actual factors behind the low procurement volume and thus pointed to a clear path to resolve this critical business problem. In short, a customized action plan could be developed with the regional managers to help flagging donor center managers build their people performance metrics. Further, leaders of top-producing centers could then be tapped to train managers in lower-producing donor centers on the strategies, tactics, and shortcuts to spike performance. (At the same time, those top donor center leaders/trainers were then identified for regional manager succession plans.)

As you can see, much of this exercise could be conducted on the back of an envelope or napkin. In this case, a simple Excel spreadsheet did the trick: donor center managers received a human capital scorecard for their center; regional managers received a spreadsheet with six tabs (representing each of their six donor centers); general managers' spreadsheets had eighteen tabs; and senior vice presidents' spreadsheets had fifty tabs. It was a relatively simple way to compare apples to apples and have donor center differences jump off the page. Here was a black-and-white tool that pointed to specific action plans for each donor center leader. And it all stemmed from the healthy curiosity and creativity on the HR team's part that connected the dots between donor center performance and human capital metrics. A goal was then set to turn around flagging centers within six months. Other ideas from donor center managers and regional leaders then emerged to create healthy competitions, bring in guest speakers, and create leadership focus groups to share best practices.

The result: leadership realignment, recognition for top-performing donor center managers who were tapped to teach their peers, a greater sense of purpose and engagement among lower-performing donor center managers who had felt frustrated and unengaged up to that point, plus concrete action plans to build critical leadership muscle in areas of the business that previously received inadequate attention. The solution—measurably improved performance, productivity, and business success in the struggling centers—did not rely on paying donors more for their blood plasma donations. Rather, it emanated directly from a reengagement of the donor centers' management teams and realignment of their interests with those of their regional leaders, general managers, and senior vice presidents. The metrics told the story. And creating a simple spreadsheet with multiple tabs made the action plans and lessons easy to identify and implement.

STEP TWO: UTILIZE DATA SCIENCE AND DATA ANALYTICS

What's the difference between HR metrics and HR data analytics? HR metrics are typically used to assess the performance, efficiency, and effectiveness of HR processes and practices and to provide snapshots into the current state of productivity and compliance. In contrast, HR data analytics are used to generate insights and knowledge that can inform strategic near-term and longer-term decision-making at the organizational level. In that sense, HR analytics take HR metrics to the next level. It's like the difference between accounting and finance. Accounting looks at the present state of things to capture where the company stands now. Finance, in comparison, projects current trends and patterns to forecast where things will likely go and what types of interventions now might influence future outcomes.

Technically speaking, HR analytics, also called people analytics, are the quantification of people factors and human capital information on business outcomes. Put plainly, analytics measure why something is happening and what the future impact may be in an effort to influence longer-term outcomes (for example, to decide on training and upskilling coursework, improve workplace processes, and promote a positive employee experience). The overarching goal of people analytics is to improve individual as well as team and organizational performance. It can help you assess broader elements, such as the employee experience and culture and general sense of employee satisfaction and engagement. HR data analytics can also be used to track and measure the effectiveness of particular programs, such as employee wellness initiatives, diversity and inclusion programs, and talent management strategies. By analyzing data in these programs, organizations can determine what is working well and what needs improvement, allowing them to make data-driven decisions and allocate resources more effectively.

You should expect to see and hear more about this throughout your career. Artificial intelligence, machine learning, quantum computing, and other developments will be applied to human capital performance to spike organizational productivity. And no, you don't need to be a math or computer science major to explore the benefits of statistical methods, algorithms, and other quantitative tools to gain insights into organizational performance. Your software programs will do the heavy lifting for you. Some commonly used tools include:

- Microsoft Excel: Excel is a widely used tool for data analysis and visualization. It has various features such as data sorting, filtering, and charting that can help HR professionals to analyze HR data.
- Tableau: Tableau is a powerful data visualization tool that can be used to create interactive dashboards and visualizations to analyze HR data.
- SAP SuccessFactors: SAP SuccessFactors is an HR management software that provides analytics and reporting capabilities to help HR professionals make data-driven decisions.
- Workday: Workday is an HR management software that provides various analytics and reporting features to help HR professionals analyze HR data.

Analytics are where data science meets people. You can expect this to become a significantly stronger driver in the people leadership space over time, regardless of the size of your organization. Just remember that while the software will do much of the back-end work in terms of data gathering, knowing what questions to ask the software is key. Developing a healthy sense of curiosity and being an "early adopter" of data analytics will surely help you throughout your career, regardless of the HR specialty you ultimately pursue.

STEP THREE: LOOK FOR QUICK WINS TO BUILD YOUR GOALS AND YOUR PERSONAL BRAND

As we shared elsewhere in this book, we know what millennials and Zoomers want when considering joining or remaining with employers, including career and professional development as well as greater control over work-life-family balance. Where can you find "strategic" opportunities to help build your department's, team's, and personal goals? How do these sound for strategic interventions:

- Install canisters in each breakroom to collect used bottles, cans, and plastics.

- Institute a program of quarterly one-on-one professional development meetings for employees to discuss progress toward their career goals, educational desires (including licensures and certificates), and aligning professional interests with project-related opportunities or exposure to other parts of the organization (including cross-training).

- Implement a suite of "selfless" benefits that help employees make the world a better place, including coworker vacation donation programs, annual community days to help causes that the company adopts, and "payroll pledge" donation opportunities to support nonprofit causes.

- Build a management training program around leading remote employees and "managing the unseen" to ensure that fully remote or hybrid employees feel connected to the organization and their peers.

- Establish a worker-led Employee Resource Group, or ERG, where employees voluntarily join based on shared identities, communities, and interests. Some examples include a working parents' group, women's network, moms-returning-to-work cohort, veterans team, and specific culture or ethnicity-based groups.

What these "strategic" programs have in common is that they specifically meet the needs of the various generations, aligning the organization's interests with what we know the generational groupings are seeking. As you can see, the potential costs for these types of programs can be minimal, yet the level of appreciation from your employees can be exceptionally high. At the very least, you'll be considered a manager who "gets it," who's not out of touch in terms of what's going on in the broader market, and who cares enough about your employees to listen to their needs and customize solutions to meet them. Now *those* are smart moves that can move the needle! And that's exactly the kind of thinking and the type of approach that CEOs and business owners are looking for from their HR leaders to help move the organization forward.

STEP FOUR: CONSIDER DRAFTING AN HR MISSION STATEMENT AND STRATEGIC PLAN

What gets measured gets managed. And what gets written down typically creates a commitment to a team goal that gets quantified, evaluated, and nurtured to completion. While you may not have full authority to launch a departmental mission statement, you can work on one with your team for your own group's focus. (Be sure to keep your manager in the loop so there are no surprises.) One key question to pose to your team is, "What are your specific thoughts regarding the philosophy, goals, and motto that best reflect our values, especially in terms of our purpose and our desired impact on the organization as a whole?" You can follow up on their responses by asking them about the ways that we can support all stakeholders, why and how we make the organization a better place, and which goals, values, and ethical drivers help us stand out. By reaching a shared understanding about what we do, how we do it, and why we do it, the next question should focus on how we build that into our departmental or team mission statement.

When it comes to building an HR strategic plan, ask deeper questions that map out your approach to solving workplace challenges and aligning HR with your stakeholders' most pressing needs. Conduct a SWOT (Strengths, Weaknesses, Opportunities, and Threats) analysis of your organization's current state of affairs to identify the context within which your solutions will lie. One central question lies in asking how can we align ourselves with our organizational vision and corporate values statement? How can we leverage HR to enhance executive business strategy? How can we improve decision-making through the use of business analytics and scenario planning? How can we adopt new technology, including artificial intelligence, to model approaches for better decision-making in periods of risk and uncertainty? Most important, which human capital metrics will help us best determine HR's return on investment and organizational impact?

Write the first drafts, review them with your immediate manager, and finalize them with senior HR leadership approval. Frame the work you do in terms of concrete, measurable objectives and goals that can be quantified quarterly in dollars and percentages, whenever possible. Simply thinking about a gap analysis that compares current HR systems with future talent requirements will help you define your work, set appropriate goals, and influence your results more positively. This is what "strategic thinking" is all about. It's a mindset that helps you see things from the thirty-thousand-foot view rather than from the weeds. It's an approach to work that helps provide a healthy perspective and constructive context within which all achievements can be rightfully celebrated. In short, it will help you ask the right questions, create proper goals, generate the desired outcomes, and demonstrate your value and accomplishments in concrete terms—truly a wise approach to a career in management and leadership!

16

EMPLOYEE DEVELOPMENT AND TALENT MANAGEMENT
Creating and Supporting a Coaching Culture

LEADERSHIP IS THE GREATEST GIFT THE workplace offers because it gives you the opportunity to positively influence others' lives and create more leaders in turn. Let's work together to build this muscle, hone this craft, and create this philosophy that helps us excel, immediately benefits those whom we lead, and provides a competitive advantage to your organization. Think of yourself as your company's greatest "talent asset"; *you* are the profit lever. Now is the opportunity to reinvent, reflect, facilitate, include, and amplify others assigned to your care. It's time to make your world bigger, to expand your line of sight, and to recognize and appreciate the awesome opportunity you hold as a leader.

THE LEADER-AS-COACH MODEL

As a leader, your success is directly measured by the success of those working on your team; their success is your success. It follows that the skills that made you successful as an individual contributor won't necessarily all apply to your role as leader. As a leader, you should strive to create a "coaching culture" that focuses on selflessness and otherness; a concern that those who report to you grow, both personally and professionally; a dedication to listening with empathy and helping people find their way through their challenges rather than just giving them answers; and a personal commitment to those who have been entrusted to you via your managerial leadership role in your organization.

You might stop right here and think, "Wait. I'm not here to be a career adviser to my people. There's work to be done, and they'll need to figure out how to be successful just like I had to figure it out. No handholding and coddling on my team—I hate to say it's sink or swim, but hey, if it worked for me, it should work for them." Let's have another look at your premise, though. While there's no right or wrong answer, it's possible that your initial reaction is a bit out of touch with the times. First, understand that millennials and Gen-Z currently make up almost half of the workforce as of this writing, and that percentage will increase dramatically as the last of the baby boomers near retirement around 2030.

What do these younger generations want? Career mentoring and professional development, corporate social responsibility and environmentalism, greater control over work-life-family balance, and a more diverse and inclusive workforce. Do those ideals sound too lofty to you to be real? They're not. They may be different from previous generations' priorities of vertical career progression and wealth attainment or even compliance with and adherence to authority and formalized corporate structures. But these values and differentiators from previous generations are valid nonetheless. In fact, they're actually healthy and well thought out, meaning that if you don't meet at least some of these needs from a corporate strategy standpoint, you may be left lacking (that is, suffering from premature turnover or lackluster performance).

Further, a quick look at the future of our workforce points to the following key trends:

- As robotics, artificial intelligence, and the gig economy grow, jobs are being reinvented, and people's expectations surrounding work, roles, and career paths are changing along with them.

- Fundamental skills such as critical thinking, problem-solving, communication, creativity, and emotional intelligence are the building blocks upon which our future economy will rely.

In short, the new economy will require knowledge workers who often know more about their work than their boss does. They'll be easier to manage if you can make room for their intellectual, social/emotional, and spiritual needs and then simply step out of the way as they find new and creative ways to complete their work. A new vision of the benefits of leadership will surely help you here.

Next, if we ignore these generational priorities, especially the first one focusing on career and professional development, we may fall prey to what Patrick Lencioni's book *The Five Dysfunctions of a Team* points out as culture and individual career killers:

1. absence of trust
2. fear of conflict
3. lack of commitment
4. avoidance of accountability
5. inattention to results

Do you really want to manage in an environment that's identified by those hallmarks? No, demographics is destiny, and this flood of early-career workers is making its priorities and prerogatives clearly known. And rightfully so: every new generational cohort gets its chance to reinvent the way work gets accomplished, and the career and professional development interests this new generation shares may drive future organizational structures and roles significantly.

Let's look at creating a coaching culture together, understanding that we can affect only our immediate areas of responsibility. Don't be surprised to find, however, that if your leadership style is generating concrete results, others will surely follow. Cultures can be changed from the bottom up—all it takes is a desire and skill set to bring workers and the work they do to the next level. Let's discuss how to do just that.

A NEW CULTURAL CONSTRUCT FOR TODAY'S WORKPLACE

Culture is a popular topic these days and for good reason: working conditions drive everything from creativity and innovation to discretionary effort and self-motivation or else lead to low performance and productivity and premature turnover. It's easy to describe what a healthy culture should look like, but it's much more difficult to attain and maintain one. Culture is simply the way an organization does things in addition to what it encourages and values. Culture encompasses leadership style, multigenerational inclusion, conflict resolution, ethics and morals, diversity orientation, strategic thinking, operational tactics, and so much more. When you get right down to it, though, it's an organization's style, philosophy, and mission all wrapped up into one big corporate personality or persona. Is your organization fun, creative, or innovative? Is it progressive, paternalistic, formal, or nurturing? Is it selfless, connected, compassionate, or judgmental? Is it easy to fit in or overtly cliquish?

The leader-as-coach model influences culture significantly. It focuses on values held by senior and midlevel management that heavily influence the work experiences of teams and individual contributors. And while you can't change the culture of your entire organization yourself, you have the power to create your own subculture in your department or team that influences all members' experiences of working at your company and, more importantly, working for you.

The leader-as-coach model creates a culture of strategic clarity, clear goals and objectives, high expectations for success, and ongoing accountability. It's based on building a relationship of trust, tapping a person's potential, building commitment, and executing goals. Coaching bases itself on the assumption that everyone can grow and that everyone has the potential to become something better, regardless of the point of departure. It focuses purposely on building trust, challenging paradigms, providing effective feedback, and listening empathically. It challenges people to reframe their point of view, find their own solutions, and set their own goals and achievement markers.

The coaching model stems from the principle of selfless leadership, where leaders put others' needs ahead of their own and expect them to respond in kind. It accepts the premise that no job is great enough for the human spirit and asks a humble question:

> How many of you believe you possess far more talent, ambition, competence, skill, and passion than your current job permits you to express?

And understanding that a majority of workers will acknowledge the limitations placed on them by time, resources, and yes—their leaders' personal shortcomings or lack of engaging work—it attempts to help those being mentored to reinvent themselves, execute their predesignated goals flawlessly, and celebrate achievements and accomplishments.

I know, it sounds too good to be true. Yet, while it's not always easy to be this type of leader to your employees, it's something to strive for. It stems from your pure concern for others' well-being. It thrives on your willingness to listen, to have someone's back, and to encourage someone to be their best self—marrying both individual career and company interests. It's about emotional intelligence, active listening, light-handed guidance in which you ask questions more than give answers, and fun and laughter. In short, it's about *otherness*.

You've likely experienced this already in your career but may not have realized it. Have you ever had a favorite boss? Did you work for someone who made you feel like your opinion mattered, who challenged you to do things you didn't necessarily feel you were ready for, or who otherwise made you somehow feel special? If so, then you had an amazing coach. That person may have been your immediate supervisor, a team leader, or a department or division head, but you can be thankful that you experienced selfless leadership firsthand. And if you haven't experienced it up to this point in your career, don't worry—you will. The question to ask yourself as you continue through this book is, how will you pay it forward? How will you become *that* person to those that follow you? Do you want to be known as a person who is excellent at growing teams, turning around flagging groups, and developing high-potential employees who may not have seen in themselves what you saw in them?

Selfless leadership, emotional intelligence, and genuine care are the ingredients needed to make a coaching culture work. Never forget, the whole world is watching you. They're watching for the gift you're about to give them. Give a gift of encouragement, genuine concern, lightheartedness, and celebration. The culture of your immediate team may not be reflected companywide, but your team will become the one that everyone wants to work on, you'll be the leader that everyone wants to work for, and results will naturally follow. That's what a coaching culture creates. That's how it changes the personality of the company over time. Best of all, it can start right here, right now, as long as you're willing to be the first domino.

A PRACTICAL EXAMPLE: DISCUSS "BEING A FAVORITE BOSS" WITH YOUR CLIENT MANAGERS

Raising your manager-clients' awareness of becoming someone's favorite boss—a prism that captures employee engagement and satisfaction, discretionary effort, and high performance—is fairly easily explained in a group setting. Ask your clients to describe the best boss they've ever had. (There's no need to mention names or companies, just attributes of what made someone their favorite boss.) You'll likely get answers like this:

- She always made me feel welcome and like my opinion mattered.
- He challenged me to do things I didn't think I was ready for. He seemed to have more faith in me than I had in myself.
- She cared about my career and professional development. It was because of her that I went to night school to finish my bachelor's degree.
- He always had a calming influence on us no matter how crazy things got. He found humor in things, helped us keep a healthy perspective, and looked for ways to surprise us and keep things fresh.

The next question is a simple one: "Are you describing that person's *beingness* or *doingness*? In other words, are you focusing on what they did or who they were?" From there, the conversation promises to get interesting. The answer, of course, is both. But if you really peel back the layers of the argument, which is it? Your client managers will likely initially agree that it's the person's doingness. It's what they *did* that made them so wonderful. But some voice in the back of the room will likely volunteer an alternative choice: It was their beingness. It was who they were that made them do what they do. And voilà—like a great executive coach, you will have teased the wisdom right out of them. The lesson, ultimately, is that it's your beingness as a leader that counts. In fact, it all boils down to two words: *character* and *caring*. That's what makes someone a favorite boss. As a society, we're constantly focusing on doing—doing—doing, to a point where our hair's on fire and we're constantly chasing our tails. But to be a great boss, you simply have to *be* a certain way. Be the calm; heal the room. And make space for your staff members to gain traction and find ways of their own to motivate themselves.

And voilà—you end up with a very quiet room of client leaders who can now sort your wisdom through their own experiences and determine how they can be that gift to others. That's what a coaching culture is all about and what it feels like. That's how you can become the best HR manager your clients have ever had: By giving people back to themselves. By building their self-confidence in leading others. And by letting them know you're there for them, you have their backs, and they can become someone else's favorite boss without losing control or respect. Then ask them to do the same with their people and pay it forward. It can be that simple.

Finally, remember that coaching bases itself on asking optimal questions, not necessarily giving people answers. To reference an old metaphor, teach your people how to fish rather than give them a fish. Ask questions like these to your budding leaders and high-potential team members:

- Would you want to work for you?
- If the whole company followed your lead, would you be happy where you took it?
- (In response to an "I don't know" answer): I know you don't know, *but if you did know*, what would your answer be?

There are many more, of course, but coaching cultures thrive on career introspection. They help employees see the bigger picture, the thirty-thousand-foot view, so they can compartmentalize and better understand the challenges they currently face. They challenge employees to do their best work every day with peace of mind and encourage curiosity and ongoing learning. And they help build confidence so that staffers feel like they're thriving and creating real value for the firm. That's the standard you want to set, that's the culture you want to perpetuate, and that's the gift you have to pass onto others. Teach them how to pay this forward in their own careers over time. Model the conduct that you want others to demonstrate, and simply watch how it returns to you.

17

MANAGING THE UNSEEN
Engaging the Remote Workforce

THE COVID PANDEMIC IN THE EARLY 2020S was an eye-opener for many unexpected reasons. But certain patterns and trends were already underway, and remote work was one of them. Remember, as we've made the case elsewhere, demographics is destiny, and Gen Y and Gen Z are the most studied generational cohorts in history. We know what they want more than we've ever known about any generations that preceded them, and work-life-family balance, control, and equilibrium were at the top of their priority list well before COVID ever entered the scene. But with so many employees working in different locations and time zones, everyone is required to communicate in multiple dimensions—live, by phone, by videoconference, email, texting, and more—which can be exhausting. For every gain in convenience and efficiency the virtual world offers, it can set us back when it comes to clear communication and the alignment of schedules and goals.

First, sociologists generally consider Gen Z to be the most isolated and depressed generation on the planet today—even more so than retirees in retirement homes. They grew up on digital technology to the point where, some would argue, technology displaced human connection. Cell phones became human extensions of their bodies—another hand or arm—and texting and instant messaging became for many the communication medium of choice. This, however, precluded human connection and fostered a sense of isolation. Further, cell phones were on all the time—including during sleeping hours at night—creating a reliance (some might call it an "addiction") to electronic stimulation, whether they were texts from friends, social media alerts, or even breaking news announcements. As such, it became difficult for certain members of this generation to "unplug." Working from home—with its ongoing 24/7 access to email and other systems—likely perpetuated this inability to disconnect. And quite naturally, this younger cohort is looking to employers to help them differentiate work from their personal lives and "disconnect" safely from work stimulation. COVID and remote work simply sped up these trends, which were already in place and gaining momentum.

For many organizations, intergenerational, geographically dispersed hybrid/remote teams are now the norm. But not for all. One fundamental question for organizations and the C-suite will remain: Should remote work be permitted or encouraged to continue in light of the changes made possible by digital technology and videoconferencing, remote systems access, and more? For some companies, the studies showing the productivity increased during COVID's remote working requirement period were enough to convince progressive employers that this new model might kill two birds with one stone—enhancing employee engagement and spiking performance.

For other organizations, the realization that business could continue to improve without brick-and-mortar office space pointed to incredible cost savings without a lot of downside risk. Still, certain CEOs and business owners suffered under what became known as "productivity paranoia" and wanted everyone back to work as if COVID never existed and put a quick stop to remote working capabilities. Those organizations might have come across as tone-deaf at the time and experienced challenging talent acquisition and retention trends during the Great Resignation, but concerns about loss of culture, camaraderie, and collaboration are valid. Only time will tell how the business world recalibrates and rebalances itself in a postpandemic reintegration phase (which, due to demographic shifts and communication technology upgrades, may last decades).

Assuming your organization continues to permit remote work, either fully or in terms of some sort of remote model, what's critical is improving remote individual and team effectiveness. True, operational leaders will worry to a degree about remote employees' engagement levels—specifically about people's accountability, lack of communication, agility, and performance. But there's a lot that can be done to improve the remote versus on-site balance. The same guidelines about great leadership remain as relevant in a remote relationship as in an on-site one: trust, respect, and honesty; communication, teamwork, and selfless leadership. The difference, however, lies in the fact that remote leadership must be more focused, intentional, and purposeful. Less can be left to chance (assuming you'll see everyone in the lunchroom or hanging around the proverbial watercooler) to catch any frustrations, distractions, or tensions. The following tips and strategies may go a long way in addressing the biggest obstacles and strengthening ties to and with remote workers, whether they are fully remote or hybrid remote:

1. Ensure that everyone remains "ever present" when working remotely. That means keeping the video screen and sound on so that participants don't get lost in multitasking activities that distract them. In short, if you can't see and hear your people at all times on a videoconference call, they're probably engaged in something else. Besides, it's a simple matter of respect to communicate with your eyes in addition to your ears when dealing with bosses and peers—remote communication should be no exception.

2. Expect participation. If, as a leader, you aren't getting the level of participation you want from your virtual meetings,

make it clear in both group and one-on-one communications what your expectations are. Guide your client managers to do the same if their meetings suffer from little participation.

3. Hold regular one-on-one weekly meetings with your direct reports. Assuming a span of control of four to eight team members, this can be broken down over a two-week period. But dedicated one-on-one time is critical to ensure full accountability, project management, goal alignment, and the need to pivot. Discuss if work ever feels like it's becoming overly depersonalized and what can be done about it.

4. Hold regular weekly/biweekly staff meetings with your full team (direct reports and/or extended reports) to ensure that everyone feels aligned and in sync. True, staff meetings take time and can sometimes be seen as a "necessary evil," but they're needed more in remote working relationships than ever before, both to build teamwork and camaraderie and also to keep everyone informed of critical changes and feeling less lonely and isolated.

5. Hold quarterly professional development meetings with your direct reports and ask them to do so with their direct reports (your extended reports). Goal attainment can change quickly in a world with competing priorities, and "annual" goals and performance review meetings are likely not enough to get you where you want to go. Make your team members responsible for scheduling those meetings on your calendar and give them full control of the agenda that they'd like to discuss. Further, keep this all about goal attainment and professional and career development—not about day-to-day operations. You can talk about the latter any time: this meeting is for building talent and leadership muscle, codifying achievements, and discussing the individual's needs.

6. Schedule occasional ad hoc meetings to conduct reviews of what's working well and what needs to be improved. You won't know unless you ask. For example, one way your team can reinvent itself is by holding a Stop-Start-Continue workshop, soliciting honest feedback regarding what you and your team need more of, less of, or to stop altogether.

7. Rely on informal check-ins to calm employee anxiety. SHRM conducted a study in 2022 that found that 50 percent of workers suffered from "Sunday Scaries" about returning to work on Monday morning. Walking around to check in and see if anyone needs anything is easy enough in person; but reaching out via short touch-base phone calls has a similar effect—stemming anxiety. Virtual assistants and "chatbots" can also be programmed to do the same thing. While lacking a human touch, technology outreach can still pose important questions like, "Do you have sufficient resources to do your job?" or "Is there anything you feel is important to share with your manager?" People are getting more comfortable with automation, and this virtual assistant option may work better than you think, especially for larger teams where personal outreach is more challenging.

8. Make professional networks and mentoring relationships part of your hybrid or fully remote success strategy. After all, career and professional development remains at the top of the list in terms of millennial and Gen Z priorities. Building on people's strengths is a core focus of every mentoring program available today, whether the organization employs full-time external executive coaches, appoints internal management mentors, assigns buddies or ambassadors to support new hires, or relies on apps to help workers better themselves. Do this especially with an emphasis on women and minorities as part of your organization's DEI (diversity, equity, and inclusion) efforts.

9. Choose the right technology tools to foster greater communication and teamwork. Most managers are unaware of the full menu options available in workspace technology platforms. For example, the right technology not only ensures excellent communication but can likewise show leaders that employees are really working by creating a virtual infrastructure that maps to physical infrastructure. This way, managers can see where everyone is, what they're working on, and who they're working with. It eliminates the need for monitoring because you can see from an employee's avatar exactly where they are and what they are doing. It can offer the benefits of in-person work without the commute and permit you to hire the most qualified talent without geographical restrictions. Cool stuff!

10. Consider creating "Personal Preference Worksheets" to allow everyone to express what works best for team members in a remote environment. Such team-building tools help staff members explicitly communicate how to best work with them, who they are as a human being (that is, what they value most), and provide others with advice and a framework on how to best communicate with them. For example, some employees who see themselves as introverted may feel at a disadvantage (relative to their more outgoing peers) in terms of expressing themselves freely over videoconference calls. This type of tool helps make others aware of their communication and collaboration preferences in an attempt to level the playing field and spike inclusion and psychological safety. Templates are available online under "Personal User Manuals" and might look like this:

PERSONAL PREFERENCE WORKSHEET (SAMPLE)
What's one "fun fact" (personal or business) that you'd like to share that others probably don't know about you?
How would you define your core values? In terms of values-based leadership, what are your top three priorities? (For example, having one another's back, creating a friendly and inclusive work environment, avoiding drama, and the like.)
Where do you have the least amount of patience? What should we be aware of in terms of potential hot buttons that we should try to avoid? Are you ever susceptible to "islanding" where you block out everything else and perceive calls and interruptions as intrusive or aggravating?
How do you collaborate best and what's your ideal mode of communication—phone, email, or chat?
What gives you energy at work? What's guaranteed to still make you smile when it comes to your job? What might drain your energy reserve the most?
Where do you sometimes feel misunderstood? What might people misunderstand about you that you'd like to clear up?
How do you like to give and receive constructive feedback? (Do you pride yourself on your thick skin, or can your feelings sometimes be hurt?) Also, do you know when *not* to work and draw appropriate boundaries?
Do you have any idiosyncrasies in your work style that you're comfortable sharing with the rest of the team? (It's okay if it's funny—laughter is a healing art!) Do you sometimes feel like you suffer from "face stress" on Zoom? When does texting work better for you than telephone calls or videoconferencing?
What subjects do you like to talk about most that don't have anything to do with work (for example, sports, the stock market, travel, and so on)?
What do we do in case of emergency? Is there an emergency shutoff valve? What will SOS look like and how can we survive? And is there anything you're focusing on to get better at remote working?

Special note: this exercise lends itself well to pairing with personality or work preference self-assessments, which can dive deeper dive into these various preferences and be used as a team-building exercise.

The hybrid world will continue to present myriad challenges. There will always be extra effort required to loop in remote workers when others are on-site. Clearly, social connections and the "psychic income" derived from work can be compromised when a mix of in-person and remote work is at hand, for no other reason than certain employees may not feel as comfortable speaking up in a remote landscape or may resent feeling left out of even small decisions. But discussing concerns openly and in one-on-one meetings becomes key in surmounting them. Open communication and information sharing take on a new meaning in the remote work world because everyone generally enjoys getting to know their peers better. Find your key concerns and communicate them broadly, asking team members to proffer solutions that will address these potential land mines and avoid potential crises. Make time to address improvements; give your team members the space and encouragement to find creative solutions. Sure, you'll have additional challenges managing remote staff, but think of the critical muscle you'll build in this new and hot area of professional expertise!

18

THE ROI OF DEI
A Mission-Critical Imperative for Developing a Diverse and Inclusive Talent Pool and Workplace Culture

DIVERSITY, EQUITY, AND INCLUSION (DEI) is a critical part of any organization's business strategy for one simple reason: talent diversity is a competitive advantage. McKinsey and other consulting firms as well as myriad business schools have confirmed that organizations with diverse boards, leadership teams, and workforces continue to outperform companies with more homogeneous employees and board constituents.

A STARTING POINT

Many organizations don't know where to begin when it comes to launching a DEI program. That's understandable because it's such a huge topic with many complexities. It's always best to start with a shared understanding of what diversity, equity, and inclusion mean, what the benefits are, and why it's important to you, your company, and community. Don't be surprised to hear about common misperceptions, including the fact that (1) DEI is only for minority groups, (2) HR is the only department responsible for DEI, (3) DEI is about hiring unqualified candidates, or (4) DEI is a "soft issue" that has little practical bearing on business performance. In fact, these assumptions are all inaccurate, as we'll explore below.

First, DEI launches begin with a leadership commitment. DEI initiatives require executive-level support to drive meaningful change. Second, an organizational "quality audit" is conducted where HR and leaders from other departments assess your DEI landscape. (These leader volunteers often become members of your DEI committee.) These analyses include language in your offer letter templates, employee handbook, policies and procedures manual, job postings, employee feedback programs, and organizational communications overall (including the website and social media) to assess the current state of the organization.

Third, conduct a "quantity audit," introducing metrics to gain an objective and dispassionate look at employment practice results. Metrics can be used to evaluate the makeup of the senior leadership team, employee population as a whole, and internal promotion and transfer rates. Note that artificial intelligence will be very helpful in taking DEI initiatives to a much higher level by improving the hiring pipeline, "blinding" the résumé screening process, assessing employee engagement and performance levels for underrepresented groups, unearthing root causes of potentially problematic practices, and launching targeted interventions into job satisfaction and productivity. AI will likewise be able to benchmark your firm against peers.

Fourth, form a diversity committee or council, first with leadership volunteers (often directors and above) and eventually with line and operational staff members. (It's typically best to start with senior management in my opinion since some of the information produced may be problematic and need to be addressed before rolling out the program to a broader employee audience.) The goal of the council is to draft a DEI goal statement and action plan, typically by quarter over the upcoming six to twelve months. The action plan should include key areas, including recruitment and hiring practices, career and professional development opportunities, training and development considerations, retention strategies, and the possible introduction of employee resource groups.

Fifth, launch DEI employee training workshops, lunch-and-learns, or off-site meetings to educate employees on what DEI is, how your organization will implement DEI initiatives, who volunteers on your DEI committee, what your core goals and means of achieving them are, and what unconscious bias, inclusive leadership, and cultural competency look like. Encourage employee feedback and participation, expect some to volunteer to participate on the council, and keep an open mind to incorporate employee suggestions to the extent possible.

Finally, measure progress toward your goals and action plan items. Accountability is everyone's job—not belonging only to HR or members of the council. Identify key metrics and indicators of success, celebrate improvements in your organizational practices, communicate frequently with employees so they're aware that a spirit of inclusion is alive and well in your organization, and attempt to raise this to an organization-wide initiative, worthy of your company's annual report. Remember that DEI is a living, breathing program, a culture and philosophy about inclusion and belonging. As such, your organizational focus on helping employees do their best work every day with peace of mind and respect can become and remain a hallmark of your leadership brand.

Likewise, progress won't necessarily be linear: expect improvements that looked promising initially to lag and areas with little activity up front to suddenly skyrocket. Understand that there may be disagreement or confusion on behalf of council members. Feelings can sometimes run high when it comes to perceptions of opportunity, advancement, and fairness, so when in doubt, err on the side of compassion and know that everyone is doing their best to make the program successful. But experiencing confusion from council members goes a long way in appreciating the challenges of rolling out a DEI initiative to all employees.

A CHECKLIST TOOL TO CAPTURE THE BROAD BREADTH OF A SUCCESSFUL DEI PROGRAM

Why would I suggest something as simple as a checklist to address an imperative that is so critical to any organization's strategic planning initiatives? Because DEI covers such a broad swath of business areas, initiating and expanding your program with the help of a template may be a simple yet effective place to start. To be sure, committing to diversity, equity, and inclusion isn't about completing a checklist at one moment in time. It's about continually challenging ourselves and others to question, become more aware of, and make an effort to understand different perspectives. Still, a checklist tool can be helpful in capturing the broad swath of areas potentially affected by your organization's commitment to DEI, as we'll see below.

We know that some of the world's most critical engagements succeed with the help of a simple checklist methodology. Airlines require that pilots employ checklists before every flight. Surgeons often prepare checklists before initiating certain complicated medical procedures. Leading executive coaches like Marshall Goldsmith in his Stakeholder Centered Executive Coaching program recommend employing checklists before each client engagement and use them themselves to ensure they're on point and covering all their bases. So whether you're analyzing employee demographics, recruitment statistics, retention and promotion records, or marketing and customer data, a checklist approach may make sense in terms of initiating and strengthening your organization's DEI programs and initiatives as well.

For example, you'll want a place to capture that your business, located in the San Fernando Valley outside Los Angeles, has an external demographic makeup like this: 42 percent Hispanic, 41 percent White, 12 percent Asian, and 5 percent Black. Why? Because you want to understand the makeup of the local community you serve and have a measuring rod against which to base

STRATEGIC HR AND THE FUTURE OF THE HR PROFESSION .195.

your employee demographic analysis. Obtaining this information is fairly easy with a simple Google search or with the help of the local chamber of commerce or economic development corporation.

Of course, DEI extends far beyond race and gender to include, among other things, age, disability, sexual orientation, low-income status, and more. That being said, establishing a baseline of the community you serve is an important contextual data point. Internal diversity metrics will then help you gain a snapshot of your own company's demographics. Finally, understanding how to attract more diverse talent pools makes for a simple baseline against which you can measure progress toward your organization's diversity, equity, and inclusion efforts. Again, this is only meant to be a launching point, as DEI is far more complex and intricate than any checklist might otherwise indicate. But if you're looking to truly delve into this critical study and analysis, benchmarking local and company demographics is an excellent place to start.

A checklist that measures human capital isn't intended to be static. It's intended to change, adapt, and evolve as new insights become available and warrant further exploration. But keeping it simple initially makes the most sense, while allowing the checklist to expand on its own as new data creates additional opportunities. Below is an example of a DEI checklist.

DIVERSITY, EQUITY, AND INCLUSION (DEI) CHECKLIST	
Local Worker and Extended Customer Demographics	Research statistics regarding your local workplace community and, more importantly, the customers and consumers you serve. Start with ethnicity, age, gender, gender orientation / LGTBQIA+*, veteran, and disability statistics, if available.

*The LGBTQ+ acronym is formed based on the following terms: lesbian, gay, bisexual, transgender, and queer. It's also common to see the acronym LGBTQQIA+ used nowadays, expanded for a clearer representation of lesbian, gay, bisexual, transgender, queer, questioning, intersex, and asexual people. The addition of the "+" symbol indicates its expansive meaning and stands for love, acceptance, and the embracing of all.

DIVERSITY, EQUITY, AND INCLUSION (DEI) CHECKLIST	
Company Workforce Statistics	Analyze your current workforce demography by location and line of business, including ethnicity, age, gender, gender orientation, veteran, disability status, and other factors that you deem appropriate.
Company Diversity Metrics	Review the following metrics for the particular aspects of diversity orientation that you're focusing on (for example, age, gender, ethnicity): (1) retention rate; (2) internal job-fill ratio; (3) promotion rate; (4) turnover percentage, including involuntary versus voluntary turnover.
Employee Life-Cycle Analysis and Talent Diversity	Measure each of the following key gateways and paths closely to determine where diversity tends to "fall off": (1) applicant sourcing, (2) interview screening, (3) hiring, (4) retention, (5) internal mobility, and (6) succession planning. Look for trends and patterns in roadblock areas and build your recruitment and retention programs as well as your exit interviews purposely around those challenges.
Recruitment Advertising Outreach Sources	Expand your typical Indeed.com and LinkedIn sourcing methods to include DiversityJobs .com, LatinoJobs.org, OverFiftyJobs.com, DisabilityJobs.net, AsianHires.com, NativeJobs.org, LGBTjobsite.com, VeteranJobs.net, BlackCareers.org, and WeHireWomen.com. Niche sites won't produce the volume of big job boards, but the quality of candidates should justify the cost of the ads.
Talent Intelligence (AI-Driven) Platforms	Talent intelligence (artificial intelligence–driven) platforms are becoming commercially available to identify internal talent and align succession planning and high potential development. AI can search for adjacent skills and focus on the potential of each individual applicant or employee. AI can mask individuals' identities and reduce unconscious bias. AI analytics can point to underrepresented groups that drop off within the hiring cycle or the internal promotion process. AI can "learn" diversity metrics to

DIVERSITY, EQUITY, AND INCLUSION (DEI) CHECKLIST	
Talent Intelligence (AI-Driven) Platforms (continued)	better achieve diversity goals, so long as they're updated, monitored, and adjusted regularly. AI is clearly a new, burgeoning technological tool as of this writing, and ensuring its accuracy and effectiveness will require keen human analysis and input, as discussed elsewhere in the book.

THE "QUALITY FOUR"

Of course, no checklist is broad enough to cover the essence and quality of your organization's hiring, retention, and promotion programs. Checklists, however, can certainly help on the quantitative side to ensure that you're touching all the bases and the key elements of a successful program. On the qualitative side, link your statistical metrics with a healthy and transparent discussion surrounding the cultural narrative and employee feedback. The following four broad categories are a good place to start:

- Workforce DEI: Hiring, retaining, developing, and promoting diverse employees
- Workplace DEI: Creating a company culture rooted in acceptance and belonging
- Marketplace DEI: Attracting and engaging diverse customers and suppliers
- Community DEI: Contributing to all parts of the community a company serves

Only a broad and holistic approach that incorporates all four stakeholders above will make for a true DEI program worthy of your organization and your employees. Developing a DEI policy and corresponding company initiatives that help achieve a truly diverse, equitable, and inclusive organization is a noble yet practical endeavor. It's proven to be a critical "must-have" for millennials and Gen-Z employees in terms of attracting and retaining talent, along with giving back to the community and corporate social responsibility. You don't need to have a perfect start—you just need to start. See if a simple checklist approach helps you build and develop your program—and your checklist template—over time to capture broader and more nuanced aspects of your organization's commitment to this critical business and personal imperative.

CREATING A GREATER APPRECIATION FOR DEI IN YOUR ORGANIZATION

With your fundamental approach in place, it's time to make the DEI spirit more palatable and real within your culture. Promoting DEI starts at the top, of course, so depending on the size of your organization and access to the president or owner level, help build out talking points about what you're doing in HR and on the diversity committee to sponsor and highlight your organization's efforts along these lines. Start with millennial and Zoomer priorities for diversity of thoughts, ideas, and voices. Move to the fact that Zoomers are testing out as the loneliest, most isolated, and most depressed generational cohort on the planet and are in dire need of a greater sense of belonging, which a DEI culture fully supports.

Ensure that DEI principles and values are reflected in your company's mission, vision, and policy statements. Encourage employees in written communications and at all-hands meetings and employee gatherings to share ideas and suggestions for making your workplace more inclusive for all. And map out how you're developing and nurturing diverse hiring practices, including advertising on boutique job boards that appeal to a diverse candidate pool, working mothers, workers over forty, military first-time jobbers, people with disabilities, and other underrepresented groups.

With a confirmed commitment from senior leadership, establish clear policies and guidelines around your organization's commitment to a spirit of inclusion. Distribute your policies in an email blast that includes your antidiscrimination, harassment prevention, and respect-in-the-workplace statements as well as your code of business conduct (if you have one). Better yet, call an all-hands meeting with your senior and operational managers first and then frontline employees to discuss what these policies mean and how you value them. Consider implementing unconscious/implicit bias training for managers. Ask your employees what their experiences are, what they would recommend we do differently as an organization, and what, if anything, they'd be willing to do to help. Announce a communication process and program for soliciting their input. A written assessment through SurveyMonkey might also make sense. (Note, though, that employees tend to be super paranoid about fear of retaliation for sharing their thoughts, even in so-called anonymous surveys, so be prepared to address how anonymity and confidentiality work in written or electronic surveys.)

With commitment, communication, and training in hand, make inclusion a part of your organizational goals. Company goals typically make up one element of every employee's goal program (along with departmental and individual goals). What gets committed to in writing—and is made part of employees' performance appraisals or bonus requirements—definitely moves things to the top of the priority list. A performance review competency or goal might sound like this:

- Encourages open communication, listens actively, and remains open to constructive feedback. Welcomes differing points of view and makes it safe for coworkers to share suggestions and recommendations without fear of censure.
- Recognizes the value of having our workforce reflect our diverse customer base.
- Welcomes diversity of thoughts, ideas, and voices.

- Views DEI as a strategic business initiative and reinforces the advantages of attracting and retaining a diverse workforce.
- Always treats subordinates and superiors with respect and supports them in doing their very best work every day with peace of mind.

Do you see how easily that can be translated into a performance review item or bonus element requirement? Just be sure there are metrics to measure progress on DEI goals and hold employees accountable for results.

Finally, here are additional options for your consideration that may be highly effective:

1. Create Employee Resource Groups (ERGs) to provide a platform for workers with similar backgrounds or interests to come together on a voluntary basis to build stronger peer relationships and networks and to share experiences.
2. Implement buddy programs for more seasoned employees to help new hires onboard more effectively (and make that the mandatory first step in any type of high-potential program).
3. Establish ambassador programs for those who want to dedicate their personal time to community interests (which are typically very well received by younger workers who look to make the world a better place).
4. Set up formal mentorship programs that can go a long way in helping younger professionals gain knowledge and wisdom from their elder counterparts.

Solicit feedback from your employees directly and adapt programs to address this critical business imperative, have fun while you're doing it, and do your share as HR management to create a truly inclusive work environment.

19

HR INFORMATION SYSTEMS AND HR'S INTERFACE WITH ARTIFICIAL INTELLIGENCE

CLEARLY, NO BOOK FOR NEWLY MINTED human resource managers would make sense without pointing to the challenges and opportunities ahead posed by artificial intelligence and the metaverse. So, yes, I saved the best for (almost) last. The ramifications of what will come from technology are hard to comprehend, let alone predict. Still, it's important that we take a deep collective breath and gain a proper perspective so as not to feel overwhelmed by all of this. Let's start first, though, with a look at HR Information Systems (HRIS) since AI will evolve into the HRIS space, and your HRIS supports your strategic efforts so much.

HRIS: BOOSTING EFFICIENCY AND COMPLIANCE

Beware: you may be entering a zone of "rubber bands and paper clips" when you join a new organization as their first-time HR manager. Not to fear: automation is becoming easier to implement and less expensive to either purchase or "rent" (via recurring monthly or annual subscription fees). And even if technology isn't in your wheelhouse, just know that your core focus should be on implementing a versatile and flexible Human Resources Information System (HRIS) or Human Capital Management (HCM) platform that can later expand to capture applicant tracking, employee and manager self-service, training, goal tracking and cascading, talent management and succession planning, workforce analytics, employee engagement and recognition, benefits administration and open enrollment, an employee handbook builder, and more.

Vendors will make themselves available at your beck and call to present you with multiple options to suit your organization's needs. When considering implementing an HRIS program, make sure it's a combined effort with a group of stakeholders who will be intimately involved with the system: finance and payroll as well as your information technology (IT) teams. For smaller organizations, the HRIS is often shared with payroll and is part of a solution offered by either your payroll service provider or your financial system, making stakeholder involvement a key to success in selecting a system.

One of the first steps in choosing an HRIS is to ensure a proper strategic fit. How well does the system support your organization's business and HR strategy? For example, does the solution support remote workers? Another strategic goal may be in creating efficiency. One effective approach to fleshing out requirements lies in evaluating the biggest headaches or most time-consuming tasks that your organization is experiencing and then choosing an application that can have the strongest impact on your firm's financial measures. Ask first, "What is the most valuable data to my business?" Ask second, "How easily accessible is the data that I'll need most?" (That is, how well does the system perform with real-time data feeds or how easy is it for you to create a report on the desired data?) Next, define your core criteria in selecting an HRIS that you can explain to your boss as well as prospective vendors, including:

- alignment with business and HR strategy and the employee experience
- compatibility with current systems and vendors (via "linkage" or "talking to" other existing systems and third parties)
- ability to custom configure or upgrade the application
- user friendliness (both in terms of providing links to other resources and overall design of the graphic user interface)
- surveying capabilities (an app that allows employees to be surveyed securely)
- collaboration features (the ability to connect employees and allow them to collaborate on projects)
- career site and applicant tracking capabilities (the ability to track applicants and current employees)
- scheduling features (ensuring that employees are in the right places, working at the right times, and assigned to the right projects)
- data security and privacy (how often the vendor backs up system data)
- mobile device / remote system access
- workforce analytics (the ability to gather data and visualize its implications) and report generation
- initial and monthly costs or annual maintenance fees
- customer support and availability

Note: If you're overwhelmed with competing priorities, look to engage an independent HR technology consultant to help you define your requirements, conduct the evaluation, and assist in the implementation. It will be budget well spent and allow you to focus on your core areas of responsibility while launching the new system.

Don't forget to ask if there is an AI component to the HRIS database under consideration where the product can evolve and learn as you use it. (As of this writing, this represents the next stage of HRIS software development and will continue to evolve.) The remaining questions can focus on the practicality and timing of implementation, HR / payroll training, and manager/employee training. Again, you're not required to be an HRIS guru or know what suite of apps will eventually become necessary to make your HRIS program soar. What's important is that you rely on qualified vendor guidance, keep things simple, and know what you want the program to be able to do for you at the end of the day. Knowing what your end state should look like (in terms of the capabilities you'll want relative to your budget) will help the consultants determine which type of HRIS features make the most sense for your organization as part of the initial contract or as add-on services later down the road.

ARTIFICIAL INTELLIGENCE (AI): OUR NEW WAY FORWARD

Next, as we transition to AI, let's start with a short history lesson to keep the meteoric rise of this scientific and workplace phenomenon in a broader perspective. The rise of generative artificial intelligence (a.k.a. "Gen AI") and its potential economic impacts dominated the headlines once OpenAI released its groundbreaking ChatGPT software back in November 2022. The news channels couldn't get enough of generative, adaptive, and other forms of AI, and suddenly massive predictions were headlining US newspapers and social media, like:

- By 2030, forty-five million Americans could lose their jobs to AI automation, representing about one-quarter of the workforce.
- By 2030, artificial intelligence could displace roughly 15 percent of workers, or four hundred million people worldwide.

- If the trend of improving tech continues along the predicted path, many experts in the field believe that, by 2060, AI capabilities will have surpassed human cognitive power.

And if all this weren't enough, entrepreneur Elon Musk famously stated that AI carries with it "the potential of civilization destruction." How's that for an eye-opener? Before we all run for the exits, let's try and conceptualize what we're actually facing within the HR space.

NEW VOCABULARY

First, whether we like it or not, we're all going to have to get used to a new vocabulary that will hopefully enrich us over time but that may intimidate us as we learn the words' meanings and the awesome power they hold over the workplace and over our lives in general:

Generative and Adaptive Artificial Intelligence	The Metaverse
Quantum Computing	Cognitive Technology
Machine Learning	Robotic Process Automation (RPA)
The Internet of Things (IoT)	Blockchain
3D Printing	Virtual Reality (VR) and Augmented Reality (AR)

And there will surely be more terms coming our way as science delves deeper into the recesses of these various software systems and digital worlds where physicality and virtual reality collide. Likewise, don't be surprised to see the creation of a new C-suite role titled CAIO—Chief Artificial Intelligence Officer—which will have different responsibilities and areas of focus from a Chief Information Officer (CIO) or Chief Technology Officer (CTO). Will this technology fundamentally change who we are and how we do things? Of course. Will it affect the world of work (as well as just about everything else)? You bet. Should we be afraid of it? Not necessarily, but we should certainly proceed with a healthy sense of caution. We know that it's safe to say that generative AI is not yet at a place where it can be 100 percent trusted to produce accurate, valid, and reliable outputs.

To many this feels like the beginning of the age of *The Jetsons* (an early 1960s animated sitcom about futurism, including electronic maids, sealed tube transportation systems, flying cars, and remote video-based communications tools). The animation lasted only one season—twenty-four episodes—but more than a half century later, it's come to represent the fantastic technological advancements of the modern age. So, yes, much is changing and bringing with it a tremendous destabilizing force. What's crystal clear is that HR professionals still need to apply their own expertise, insights, and critical analysis to this information.

NEW ROLES

The top in-demand jobs according to the World Economic Forum's 2023 "Future of Jobs Report" include:

- AI and machine learning specialists
- sustainability specialists
- business intelligence analysts
- information security analysts
- prompt engineers (the English language is becoming the ultimate programming language since smart technology could do much of the coding for us)

Analytical thinking and creative thinking remain the most important skills for workers as of this writing. But there are significant downsides as well.

AT-RISK JOBS

The majority of the fastest declining positions will likely be clerical or secretarial roles. Bank tellers, postal service clerks, cashiers and ticketing agents, and data entry staff are expected to decline fastest, particularly in traditional security, factory, and commerce industries. The demise of white-collar professions is what you'll likely read about in the headlines. Just remember that mundane tasks and routine jobs have been disappearing for decades in light of new technologies, robots, and IVR (interactive voice response) or chatbots that effectively handle customer support for information and complaints. What generative AI has done is accelerated these developments.

But here's an important consideration and perspective: the scare of losing jobs to AI could be compared with the time when robots came onto the scene in the automobile industry in the 1960s. Prototype robots "learned" to perform spot-welding operations, and Victor Scheinman created the Stanford Arm, a programmable six-jointed robot. The same fears that robots would take over people's jobs occurred then as well, but in fact, we see more jobs today than before, many of them richer and better paying, increasing the wealth and well-being of our workforce. So, yes—jobs will be eliminated, and new jobs will be created, but they won't occur evenly or simultaneously—causing worker angst and concern and workforce disruption.

IMPACT ON THE HR WORLD

As I wrote in my book *Workplace Ethics: Mastering Ethical Leadership and Sustaining a Moral Workplace* in 2022, it is the work of humans to ensure that data remains bias free and ethically acquired. We must view AI as an enhancement tool to identify what you otherwise might have missed—not as a means and end to itself. And remember that AI should be leveraged to augment—not replace—the human experience. Ethics cannot be set on autopilot. "There's an app for that" is not an appropriate response to the many responsibilities that human resource managers will have regarding the responsible use of AI in the workplace and the impact that new technologies will have on employees' lives.

On a more practical level, it is likely that human resource managers will undoubtedly have to grapple with considerations like:

- Do you see a need for new or enhanced policies in light of the AI revolution? For example, do you intend to limit employee access to chatbots or otherwise discipline workers for plagiarism? (Or is access to AI merely equivalent to providing workers with calculators and spreadsheets?) Having clear policies in place about trade secrets, personal information, and Gen AI will become important so that no one inadvertently causes a data privacy breach.
- Will new technologies become available to master human capital metrics and analytics, especially since most human resource professionals are not schooled in the evaluation of data analytics, don't know how algorithms work, and often don't possess the technical acumen to evaluate these new, growing technologies?
- What projects or initiatives might make sense now to align your department with these emerging trends or position your department to take advantage of rapid changes in HR technology in the future (for example, deploying a new digital employee experience, implementing an AI-powered HR information system, learning management system, or applicant tracking system)?
- Where can you leverage AI-empowered solutions today that represent smaller, low-risk improvement opportunities (for example, smarter employee recognition solutions, electronic employee handbooks, and benefits information)?
- What new theories of law may emerge under the law of unintended consequences that will surely be exploited by

the plaintiffs' attorneys? Do you see lawsuits for "failure to hire" or "failure to promote" coming your way under the heading of "disparate impact" based on skewed data and misaligned algorithms?

- What does it mean—and how will you measure—the new skills and competencies required to compete effectively, including resilience, flexibility and agility, motivation and self-awareness, and curiosity and lifelong learning?

- Should your organization consider implementing AI tools to monitor your (remote) employees' daily productivity? What about using aggregated data to scrape emails in an attempt to determine who may be dissatisfied with their positions or possibly looking to jump ship? Is it too Big Brother–like and does it violate workers' trust? Does it represent an invasion of employees' privacy, especially if you take adverse action against someone—namely, termination—based on these AI findings?

- The metaverse is the emerging 3-D-enabled digital space that uses virtual reality, augmented reality, and other advanced internet and semiconductor technology to allow people to have lifelike personal and business experiences online. What can that potentially mean for your employee relations, employee wellness, and employee experience practices?

- Intellectual property (IP) can be placed at risk easily if a company permits its confidential data to get pulled into and learned by an AI system. Likewise, companies can take IP from other organizations unknowingly via AI if they are not careful. How can your company remain cautious about confidential or propriety data that should be shielded from AI exposure?

- What are the key ethical considerations that you foresee in terms of implementing AI in the workplace? Do you suspect that AI might stifle creativity and innovation since it "thinks for itself"? Are you concerned about "moral de-skilling," where senior leaders delegate their decision-making capacity to technology?

- Are you hesitant to "train AI" using your own company data? After all, there could be data security and privacy issues once your data is embedded into an AI infrastructure unless you have an ironclad understanding of where your company data may end up. Different AI tools may do different things with parcels of information, so it's important to understand specifically how the tools you're using will use that confidential organizational data.
- What concerns do you have regarding greater government regulation, labor union involvement, litigation, and the like?

Clearly, the list of concerns is long and will no doubt get longer. There's no doubt a lot here for global industry as a whole. Rest assured, however, that technology's impact on the human experience will likely create new highs and lows, helping organizations grow faster but become subject to legal challenges at every turn.

My best advice: remember that leadership is a team sport. There's no need to go it alone. Coordinate your efforts with your boss, department head, and legal counsel to ensure consistency and alignment every step of the way. Remember that the technology works from the bottom up, starting with more mundane and repetitive activities. It may take years or decades before it reaches its full potential. Your job is to protect the organization from unwanted liability, ensure a healthy employee experience to the degree possible, and model the changes coming your way. That's no easy task, but every discipline in the business world will be affected significantly. Remember that your clients are your managers and employees and that technological disruption affects them, both from a professional and personal standpoint. Involving them in where or how to automate or deploy AI will help ensure ownership and guide efforts to identify optimal solutions. You're the heart and soul of the organization—you embody the culture. Ensure that humanity doesn't suffer, that collaboration and open communication thrive, and that trust can prevail, despite the many changes and challenges coming our way.

Beyond that, expect to see potential impact coming your way in the following ways and areas.

RECRUITMENT AND TALENT ACQUISITION

AI will be able to analyze job descriptions, identifying bias or gendered language that should be upgraded. It can automate repetitive tasks like résumé screening, candidate contact, interview scheduling, and the like. It will be able to hide candidates' names and other identification elements to shield hiring managers from any sort of preconceived notions or biases that names alone can sometimes muster. In addition to reducing unconscious bias in candidate selection, AI software will be able to identify potential based on candidates' or existing employees' personal or professional interests, community involvement, and other criteria that the human eye typically misses (even where work experience may be lacking). This can expand talent pools and create opportunities for candidates and companies that extend beyond what's on a résumé.

ONBOARDING AND TRAINING

AI-powered chatbots and virtual personal assistants may be assigned to provide more personal and tailored onboarding experiences. This includes guiding new hires through the orientation process, company history, markets served, goals and potential threats, and other relevant areas that can be customized to the level of hire involved. Likewise, AI can make meaningful differences in the training and professional development space, recommending personalized learning paths and identifying professional growth opportunities. It can help workers find appropriate programs that marry their personal career interests to your organization's special needs, upskilling opportunities, and furthering the sense of a "continuous learning environment."

PERFORMANCE MANAGEMENT AND EMPLOYEE RELATIONS

AI tools can be used to assess employee performance, engagement, and substantive contributions to the team and organization. Generative AI can analyze employee feedback from surveys, performance reviews, social media, and other sources. Suggestions can be made for performance improvement and better alignment with team goals and company objectives, all leading to higher performance achievement and job satisfaction. HR analytics represents the future of HR as companies look to gain deeper insights into employee motivation and engagement. AI will stand out in this area as new analytical tools and apps become available to predict trends, patterns, and strategies regarding workforce planning, employee retention, succession planning, and other workplace considerations. Likewise, AI can help ensure compliance with safety initiatives and policy adherence, flagging any areas of potential compliance risks (think class action wage and hour lawsuits) and targeting interventions to address them.

EMPLOYEE WELLNESS AND WELL-BEING

AI-powered chatbots and virtual assistants can provide workers with 24/7 support regarding their personal goals, including weight loss, better sleep, calmness, exercise, and so much more. Monitoring employee well-being is likely one of the key areas where AI will shine because it extends company care to individuals' customized needs. One area for consideration: mental health awareness is so important today because of the social loneliness caused by the digital revolution (particularly affecting Gen-Z Zoomers). Bots may be able to provide companionship, which sounds good at first, but the longer-term effects of relying on artificial intelligence for companionship may be a significant cause for concern and become one of most significant threats and challenges from AI.

As with all things new—and especially technology with such world-changing potential—expect the law of unintended consequences to kick in at every step. Algorithms are only as good as the instructions entered at the outset. The "learning" that takes place from predictive AI can go seriously wrong—and fast—if initial "instructions" contain significant lapses in judgment or missed awareness. Human oversight is required on an ongoing and vigilant basis to ensure that the feedback, recommendations, and strategies being generated from AI are practical and have no harmful effects. Human judgment, curiosity, and empathy still rule the day.

Bottom line: tread carefully when using generative AI tools. We're very much at the experimentation phase as of this writing. HR professionals still need to bring their expertise and insights to bear to get the most out of these tools. And they need to be able to identify when the results they get appear incorrect or misleading. AI is a tool for data analysis, but it's not the analysis itself. Generative AI technology will be good at refining data—making it clearer, simpler, and easier to understand. But the technology and the information it can generate are no substitute for actual knowledge or experience that human beings add to the equation.

20

PUBLIC SECTOR HR
Human Resource Management
in Public Administration

IF YOU'RE CONSIDERING A CAREER PATH in public sector HR or already find yourself in the government sector, there are significant differences from a private sector HR career path that you should be aware of. The Public Sector HR Association, or PSHRA.org, is the public sector equivalent of SHRM. PSHRA is a leading international community for human resources professionals in the public sector, providing resources, opportunities, and advocacy to advance the public sector HR profession. PSHRA offers two professional certification programs: the IPMA-CP certification for entry-level and midcareer public sector HR professionals and the IPMA-SCP certification for senior-level public sector HR professionals. Like SHRM, PSHRA holds an annual conference and publishes its own *HR News Magazine*. A quick view of their website points to areas of focus that, like their private sector counterparts, address many of the same core leadership practices that drive private sector organizations, from administration and compliance matters to strategic HR initiatives that advance the profession and workplace in general.

What's different, however, is the culture, organizational focus, and approach to conducting business. For example, public sector organizations (county and state governments or airports, for example) are funded by tax dollars. As such, there are more regulations, controls (for example, required approvals), reporting, rules, and processes involved in typical business operations. Further, compared to private sector HR, public sector HR practices aim more at equal employment opportunities and defined career ladders, promotions, and pay increases based on seniority and less on practices aimed at appraisal and performance (such as a pay-for-performance culture). Why? Because the general public expects role-model behavior from public sector organizations funded directly by tax dollars, including diversity and inclusion efforts, equality of opportunity, and in certain states, affirmative action. (Note that some proprietary departments generate their own revenue but are still bound by the processes and controls of the public sector.) Public sector HR grounds itself on the principle of the "dignity of labor"—treating employees with respect, labor-management cooperation, and a general spirit of teamwork and cooperation among employees.

These unique characteristics require that public sector employees adhere to the tenets of public administration, civil service, political dynamics, and the diverse needs of the communities they serve. For example, public sector HR is driven by a strong focus on public service and social impact. In recruitment, specific outreach efforts to diverse and minority communities are a priority. In terms of career development, civil service job classifications and internal job examinations determine how to grow one's career over time and prepare for future advancement opportunities. Civil service systems (the term *civil service* refers to government employees in permanent public service roles) are designed to provide stability, hiring processes designed to favor internal civil service candidates, and rules governing promotion, discipline, and termination. Likewise, union influence can be high, making it difficult to terminate, for example, due to grievance and arbitration challenges.

In a unionized public sector environment, the focus on seniority as the primary driver of hiring, promotions, and pay increases has the potential to water down key organizational initiatives such as growth, innovation, agility, performance rewards, and employee engagement levels.

Government mandates and regulations can make public sector HR feel more bureaucratic, slowing down company decision-making processes. Well-defined policies relating to employment, labor relations, civil service, and public administration often have to be followed closely, allowing less room for exceptions or employer discretion. That being said, such regulations often aim to ensure fairness, consistency, transparency, and accountability in all HR practices relating to management, hiring, and discharge. Likewise, due process requirements minimize arbitrary decisions to terminate employees.

The political environment weighs much heavier on public sector employers than their private sector counterparts. A new mayor, for example, might mean change at the top of the various agencies and bureaus that serve a city or county, disrupting operations and leading to turnover in key personnel. Likewise, political agendas can have a significant impact on HR practices, such as recruitment priorities, workforce planning, and resource allocation. (Think the #MeToo, #BlackLivesMatter, #TimesUp, #HeForShe, and #OrangeTheWorld movements in addition to trends in eliminating gun violence and homelessness as well as environmentalism and global warming.)

Public service HR managers are likewise required to be familiar with non–civil service personnel because of contracting, the use of outside consultants, and the like. Larger organizations or government systems frequently have decentralized modes of HR in which a central human resource management agency sets policies, and freestanding agencies have specialized human resource departments to implement those policies and turn them into consistent practices. On occasion, agencies will have multiple specialized HR units responding to the different needs of employee groups. This "layering effect" is relatively unique to HR in the public sector and can lead to the perception of bureaucracy.

Special note: larger public service organizations are centralized in key areas, including recruitment, compensation, job classifications, promotion, controls/approvals, and union collective bargaining. These are key operational areas that must be centralized to maintain the integrity of the civil service system and to serve key public service stakeholders (employees, unions, public officials, community members, and the like). Public sector departments, in comparison, are decentralized as to employee training and development, for example, so that individual departments can build and sustain their own culture.

Employment, compensation, and training remain the three pillars of HR services in many public sector enterprises. The shared-service model, where HR functions as an internal consulting service, is becoming more common. Here HR specialists offer services to varying parts of the organization, with charges going to the functional areas receiving those HR services. It's not uncommon for HR to be combined with other staff units under an executive director of some sort (for example, an assistant city manager or deputy mayor). From a cultural standpoint, public sector HR is often structured around hierarchy, the micro division of labor, specialization, and well-defined chains of command with an emphasis on structure, rules, and finding the "one best way" to accomplish things. Auditors, investigators, and inspectors are employed to enforce standards and ensure compliance. Likewise, the news media, special interest groups, and the public need access to information to ensure that the public's rights and the common good are served and protected.

Creating and sustaining a culture of openness, careful record-keeping, and compliance with full disclosure and sunshine requirements (that is, the mandate to ensure that citizens understand the logic and reasoning behind public sector decisions that are paid for by tax dollars) lends itself to the transparency standards adopted by most public sector employers. Expect to be trained on and to train others on ethics and codes of conduct. That being said, many public employers are moving, albeit slowly, toward implementing performance management standards, performance appraisals, outcomes-related measures and goals, and continuous improvement, which are more in line with their private sector kin. Labor relations efforts focus on productive partnerships between management and unions to better support the workers being served by both.

Finally, while public sector HR managers face many of the same challenges as their private sector counterparts—hiring and retaining workers, employee satisfaction, "quiet quitting," regrettable turnover, and the like—an additional continual problem is the perception that public sector jobs underpay relative to the private sector. And while it's not always the case that public sector employers pay less than their private sector counterparts, there are situations where public sector employers simply can't match the compensation and benefits packages that for-profit firms offer. In the current race to win over top talent, even highly motivated public departments may find that they can't move as nimbly to adjust salary offerings, or be as flexible with other benefits, as less constrained private firms can.

That being the case, public sector employers have a secret weapon that leaves their private sector brethren in the dust: defined benefit pension plans, which have gone the way of the dinosaur in many private sector organizations. The value of traditional defined benefit pension plans (where workers generally do not contribute but their employer sets aside money to invest on their behalf for a retirement payout determined by an individual's age, years of service, and vesting requirements) is tremendous. Saving for retirement through 401(k) and 403(b) plans offered by employers in the private sector—known as defined contribution plans—puts the burden on workers to finance their retirement (with the help of matching-fund incentives from the employer). A quick Google search will tell you that most Americans don't have nearly enough in retirement savings to retire comfortably. Defined benefit pension plans like the ones offered in many public sector entities, in contrast, can provide a steady monthly income (like an annuity) in retirement to live comfortably for as long as you live.

In such cases, the key is to play up the benefits that public sector employers offer. Literally map out how much that pension payout will be worth in inflation-adjusted dollars after twenty, thirty, or forty years of service. Explain how taxation works. Draw comparisons to how much someone would need to pay out of pocket for an immediate annuity to generate that stream of lifetime income in retirement. For example, once employees understand that it would cost them $100,000 today to purchase an immediate annuity that pays $500/month in retirement, they'll have a much greater appreciation of their $3,000/month pension payout when they hit thirty years of service at age sixty-five. Make those numbers real to employees because there are few programs that can motivate workers to that degree.

Likewise, another key selling point for public sector employment lies in job security that is far greater than private sector, at-will employment. The civil service system and unions (through collective bargaining agreements) provide increased job security in the form of defined career ladders/paths and regular salary increases based on seniority or other non-job-performance-based factors (for example, achieving a college degree). Additionally, the civil service system and unions create job rights, including protections against termination via a high burden of proof to establish cause for termination and in favor of job reinstatement after termination.

In addition, selling the sense of service that working within the community provides is yet another highlight that helps public sector employers compete. In fact, it's this appeal to a sense of service and of working within a community that can be a uniquely compelling selling point for public sector positions. Remember that Gen-Y millennials and Gen-Z Zoomers highly value corporate social responsibility and environmentalism. They want to work for an employer that makes the world a better place. The work of the public sector is crucial, and the pandemic only highlighted for many job seekers just how vital the roles that local government employees, public safety officers, health-care workers, and social service providers are in supporting our collective well-being. Combined with the public service mission, richer defined benefit retirement plan, and enhanced levels of job security, public sector employers have much to be proud of and compete on. Simply stated, sell your mission, help candidates understand how you keep society running, and invite them to apply their talents in service of it. That's a strong combination of elements to convince people to join—and stay—with their public sector employers.

21

MERGERS AND ACQUISITIONS AND INTERNATIONAL HR
Opportunities to Explore and Room to Run

FOLLOWING ARE SOME OF THE REMAINING larger-scale HR disciplines that we won't be able to pursue in detail but that you should be aware of. Educate yourself further in these disciplines as needed, which will likely come your way as you progress through your leadership career. And keep an eye out for new trends coming your way.

MERGERS AND ACQUISITIONS HR

HR managers and practitioners in private equity are often called upon to conduct due diligence of a prospective target company's HR practices. It's a classic "buyer beware" situation: if you purchase or acquire a company, you buy all of its outstanding liabilities. This could include pending employment-related litigation, class action wage and hour exposure, underfunded pension liabilities, massive regulatory irregularities, and more. HR managers in this space are trained to conduct prepurchase due diligence to ferret out any fundamental flaws in the target company's people practices. As such, private equity HR is its own specialty discipline, and a lucrative one at that.

But mergers, acquisitions, and integrations (generally referred to as "M&A") affect all organizations from time to time—not just private equity firms that make a practice of buying and selling portfolio companies. Industry giants consolidate for myriad reasons, and we know many household names that have been through this successfully: Disney + Fox, Discovery + Time Warner, CVS + Aetna, and Dow Chemical + DuPont, just to name a few. And their reasons vary widely, including industry consolidation, value creation (that is, revenue generation and stock price increase), market share expansion, market diversification, acquisition of particular intellectual property, and tax advantages. And while all may be noble or critical justifications for M&A, the workers of those organizations—whether on the purchasing or acquired side of the equation—undergo tremendous amounts of stress, uncertainty, concern about job elimination, and much more. That's where you come in as the HR manager—the voice of reason, the calming hand, and the change leader.

One definite and often-cited benefit of a merger or acquisition lies in streamlining costs by eliminating duplicative staff functions (think HR, finance, IT, distribution, security, and other areas that can serve more in a "shared services" type of structure). But many M&A transactions are risky ventures that do not end well. In fact, according to most studies, between 70 and 90 percent of acquisitions fail. Most explanations for this depressing statistic emphasize problems with integrating the two parties involved, cultural mismatch, due diligence or deal structure error, external market factors, or failed postmerger integration.

Beyond these cultural mismatches, there may be more practical reasons why M&As fail, including disparate remote work policies, differences in pay rates and vacation policies, and variations in workforce composition and roles (that is, hourly versus salaried, professional versus trades). And management philosophies on leadership, communication, and team building may vary greatly and cause undue stress during postmerger integrations. In fact, sometimes the biggest hurdles are not what you would expect. International compensation and benefits issues, especially for expats, can cause huge liabilities. Likewise, evaluating the rates and types of typical, low-level employee-relations complaints may point to systemic problems like pervasive harassment that a company will inherit with the purchase. Whatever the reason, layoffs are often a natural outcome of merger and acquisition activity. In fact, some industry experts estimate that roughly 30 percent of employees are deemed redundant when firms in the same industry merge.

As such, M&A represents a unique opportunity for disruption in your career. The core question is, what is your leadership role when you learn of potential M&A activity coming your company's way, and what purpose do you serve in the HR suite? First, remember that while a layoff may impact you, it's not a given. Even if that does occur, it typically provides for a severance package and leaves you with an excellent "reason for leaving" your current company and initiating your job search. Layoffs have become more of a rite of passage these days because they're so prevalent, and adding M&A postmerger integration experience to your résumé prior to a layoff can give you a significant leg up on your competition moving forward in your career because most employers consider it tremendously valuable experience.

What's interesting about purchases and mergers is that you'll never know which merged department "wins out" in the end. For example, it may be the acquiring company's or the acquired company's HR team that remains when all is said and done. Just because you're officially a member of the acquiring company (versus the acquired target company) doesn't mean that your department is safe. It can likewise be a combination of both HR teams. Read that: It's important that you step up at times like these. Be the leader to unite, the positive voice of encouragement, and the eager professional looking to show the newly combined entity what you've got. Make yourself part of the renewed organizational structure. Be willing to give up your turf and assume new responsibilities in a different area. And volunteer to support the change effort in any way you can.

Most important, understand that cultural integration challenges are one of the top reasons why recently merged companies fail. Therefore, make that your key focus as you move through the integration process over that first year. It's safe to expect resistance to change from employees, communication breakdowns, misalignment of teams, leadership challenges, turf wars from senior executives, system and process misalignment, loss of customer loyalty and market share, and more. (That's why challenges like these are so valuable to your career and résumé—they demand resilience, adaptability, communication, leadership, and team-building skills.) To mitigate the risks associated with misaligned cultures, get ahead of the curve by volunteering to participate in cultural integration initiatives or develop a comprehensive integration plan that addresses the need for open and transparent communication, systems analysis, and "combining forces" by getting to know your new counterparts.

In short, don't necessarily run as soon as you hear the words *merger* or *acquisition*, whether you're on the buying or acquired side. Each crisis brings with it untold opportunities, and this could be your chance to shine in the newly formed entity. And even if it ultimately results in a layoff, think of all the credibility you'll have garnered in terms of your career trajectory. There's a reason why M&A HR is so highly valued in terms of career experience: rarely do you get the opportunity to prove your leadership acumen and solve problems on such a large-scale basis. Expect plenty of tales and stories to emerge as you learn this exciting side of corporate life. And while you may not hope to relive it any time soon, the benefits from your experience will likely give you a leg up on your competition for the rest of your career.

INTERNATIONAL HR

Did you know that Japan offers monthly menstruation leave for female workers to use as needed? In the Middle East, employees may receive tax-free salaries and other perks, including housing allowances and transportation benefits. In India, employees may be granted multiple "allowances"—all taxed at different rates and usually at a lower rate than straight income—for transportation, clothing, and lunch. Some countries pay thirteen months per year while others pay fourteen. Try this one on for size: If inflation skyrockets 40 percent in Brazil, does that mean that you should award all employees a 40 percent cost-of-living adjustment just to keep up? And what about during periods of deflation: Will you ask employees to give you your money (that is, their salary) back? Oh, and don't forget about "acquired rights." For example, in France, if you award a bonus or other benefit more than three years in a row, workers may demand that you continue it in perpetuity. (Employers must therefore stipulate in writing each year that a bonus or other benefit is a onetime event.)

"Right to work" laws may be a topic for attention globally, especially in countries like France, Brazil, and the Netherlands, which cannot only negate a termination but even reinstate workers who have been convicted of criminal activity. Also worth noting is the significant rise in the use of "global employers of record," that is, organizations that will payroll your people overseas, especially if they are in small numbers or are contractors. This is a way that smaller companies hire global talent without needing expensive immigration procedures to import workers into a new country. It likewise provides some limited shielding for small companies from onerous termination costs in those countries.

Conducting HR in a multinational context is an eye-opening subdiscipline of the broader HR profession and a specialty area unto itself. It incorporates regulatory, legal, and social mores that make each nation and company unique. Errors can be costly in this space, so finding qualified legal counsel in terms of international employment lawyers, immigration attorneys, and international CPAs is critical to your program's success. The following are some broader considerations that you should be aware of in the international arena should your new HR manager position take you there.

IMMIGRATION AND NONIMMIGRANT VISAS

Immigration is a world unto its own. The ins and outs of temporary work visas, lawful permanent resident status, applying for US citizenship, and more are time consuming and fraught with exceptions. Read that: a qualified immigration law firm is worth its weight in gold when it comes to getting international workers into the United States.

The US immigration system is divided into two groups: (1) nonimmigrants and (2) immigrants.

Nonimmigrant categories are for people who wish to come to the US for a temporary stay, for vacation, to attend school, or for temporary employment. In comparison, *immigrant* categories are for those who wish to live permanently in the United States.

For a temporary or nonimmigrant visa to be valid, candidates must establish that they have a residence in their home country that they will not abandon.

Common nonimmigrant visa categories include:

F-1 STUDENT	• The F-1 visa is usually granted for the period of time in which the student is pursuing a full-time course of study, including engaging in practical training, plus sixty days to prepare for departure from the US. This is referred to as "duration of status." • Generally, foreign students are not allowed to work in the United States. One of the requirements for a student visa is that the student proves that enough funds are available to pay for their education for the duration of studies. But there are several ways that foreign students can work in F-1 status, including on-campus employment, curricular practical training, and off-campus employment due to urgent financial need.

H-1B ALIENS IN SPECIALTY OCCUPATIONS	• Sponsoring employers are responsible for determining the "prevailing wage level," typically through published salary surveys. • Sponsoring employers must be able to show that employing a foreign national will not adversely affect the working conditions of other, similarly situated US workers. Foreign nationals must also be paid a prevailing industry standard. • Approval can be granted for an initial period of three years. Extensions of H-1B status can be obtained routinely for an additional three years. (The maximum H-1B stay is six years; seven if a green card application is in place.) • Spouses and minor children are issued H-4 visas, which are generally not valid for employment in the United States, unless an application for permanent residence has commenced and reached a certain stage. • Note that new H-1Bs are subject to a random lottery for advanced and nonadvanced US degree holders. The lottery registration period and selection draw occur in March, and those selected can apply for the H-1B starting April 1. If approved, the H-1B becomes effective in October of that year. Lottery registration and selection is subject to limits set by Congress.
J-1 EXCHANGE VISITORS	• J-1 visas are available to aliens who will be participating in an Exchange Visitor Program, including experts, foreign students, industrial and business trainees, medical interns and residents, as well as scholars. • Exchange visitor programs allow aliens to pursue education, training, research, or to teach in the United States. • If subject to the two-year foreign residency requirement, the J-1 alien must return to their home country for two years after they complete their stay in J-1 status. This is known as the "two-year foreign residency requirement." Not all J-1s are subject to this requirement. • The J-1 visa is usually issued to coincide with the length of the J-1 program (generally, eighteen months).
L-1 INTRACOMPANY TRANSFEREE	• L-1 visas are granted to aliens who have worked for a parent, subsidiary, or affiliate company abroad for more than one year as executives, managers, or in a "specialized knowledge" capacity for a total of twelve consecutive months within the immediately preceding three years. • The initial petition can be approved for up to three years with extensions granted in two-year increments, up to seven years in total.

There are other types of nonimmigrant visas (for example, E-3 work visas for Australians and TN-1 and TN-2 visas for those from Mexico and Canada), each requiring specific filing requirements, return home provisions, and the like. Your immigration attorney will be able to guide you through the process, file on your employee's behalf, or set you up to manage specific aspects of the process on your own.

Immigrant visas and permanent residency, labor certifications, and naturalization may follow. Only a limited number of immigrant visas are issued each year. This limitation is called the "quota" and is based on an alien's country of birth (not country of current residence). Immigrant visas follow what is known as a "preference system" and are grouped into two general categories: (1) family-sponsored preferences and (2) employment-based preferences (that is, applicants who have permanent offers of employment, including those with advanced degrees and extraordinary ability in the arts, sciences, business, education, and athletics). Labor certification may be required for permanent residency. Aliens may elect to become citizens through the process of naturalization, which entitles them to the right to vote, serve on a jury, obtain a US passport, and sponsor relatives for permanent status.

DOING BUSINESS ABROAD: HIRING AND FIRING

If you have a company presence in multiple countries, be sure to focus on the practices and differences in the following key employment areas:

- individual employment contracts (including trial periods and termination indemnities)
- collective bargaining and other forms of employee representation
- redundancy notice requirements and employee dismissal

- wage and hour law as well as recognized leaves
- antidiscrimination and protected groups
- pensions and benefits

Likewise, the most common questions that will likely come up on a country-by-country basis include:

- Must an employer list job vacancies with a regional labor bureau?
- Can an employer dismiss a worker without warning or notice?
- Can an employer dismiss a worker without the union's or work council's advance approval?
- Does an employer have the right to know if a particular employee belongs to a union?
- Must a works council exist in a company of a certain size, or is it a voluntary option?
- Do any laws or regulations mandate pregnancy, childbirth, and/or family leave?
- Must employers pay into a state plan ("scheme") for employee pensions?

Here's a smattering of practices that demonstrate how European Union members approach "redundancies" (that is, layoffs and downsizings):

- National laws and regulations typically stipulate a redundancy pay formula based on age and length of service. (Notice that age is a specific criterion that determines the amount of money someone receives, assuming that older workers will have a harder time finding reemployment. That's very different from in the United States.)
- The UK requires that the redundant worker receive a specific redundancy payment from the company according to a statutory formula.

- Germany requires that a works council be informed and consulted on planned redundancies prior to a worker being dismissed.
- In France, the employer is obliged to consult with the Ministry of Labor and to receive approval before mass redundancies could take place.
- Note that each European member state must implement the EU's "collective redundancies" directive via its own national legislation.
- If an employer is contemplating a redundancy action to which the directive would apply, it is required to begin consultations with the workers' representatives with a view to reaching an agreement. Works councils typically fulfill this function. Unions are permitted to strike in support of a bargaining position; works councils are not.
- The directive obliges the employer to supply works council representatives with "all relevant information" relating to the proposed redundancies.
- The company must also notify the relevant public authority of the proposed redundancies. The employer may not put the redundancies into effect until thirty days after the relevant public authority has been notified.
- The collective redundancies directive is, in some senses, merely procedural. There is no substantive restriction on companies' abilities to make workers redundant. But it does inject a consultation phase into the decision-making process preceding the implementation of redundancies. Likewise, if procedures are violated, remedy provisions for "unfair dismissal" claims include reinstatement with back pay.

Fascinating, isn't it? And that's just Europe! Each nation develops its own policies and practices based on its values, politics, history, and so much more. Without a qualified attorney to guide you through downsizings in Europe and elsewhere, however, it would be easy to step on land mines, pay hefty fines, and possibly even have to reinstate workers who were laid off. Proceed with caution, but keep these differences in mind when approaching staff changes internationally.

WORKS COUNCILS AND LABOR UNIONS

When it comes to collective bargaining, the European Union recognizes the legitimacy of unions as workers' chosen representatives and recognizes the European Trade Union Confederation as the official workers' voice in the "social dialogue." But the EU does not attempt to "harmonize" collective bargaining in the member states, so union membership, union organizing, collective bargaining, and the use of "economic weapons" varies greatly among member states. A dual channel system of employee representation exists:

A worker can voluntarily join a union.

A works council may represent a worker on many workplace issues (typically limited to one company or one workplace), especially prevalent in Germany and the Netherlands. The size of the works council is from three to thirty members; the works council has the right to meet with senior management once a year and to be informed and consulted on the progress of the business.

The EU ensures "information and consultation rights"; that is, workers are informed and consulted about events that concern them. This includes information regarding

- the state of the company;
- the introduction of new technology; and
- the markets for the company's products and services.

Companies are consequently obligated to disclose pertinent information and consult with employees' representatives *before* any planned action is undertaken. Such "transparency practices" are relatively rare in the United States by comparison, making it much more difficult to effectuate change that permits companies to downsize quickly, when needed. In comparison, Latin America generally has less regulated requirements regarding corporate actions that may affect workers, yet Brazil is known for having arcane and difficult worker protections. Now add Canada, India, Eastern Europe, Asia, the Middle East, and Africa to the mix, and you'll soon realize you're in for a real learning curve on the international front!

CONCLUSION
An Elevated Discipline and Professional Role for Twenty-First-Century Business

THE FIRST-TIME MANAGER: HR IS MY seventeenth book, and it was likely the most challenging to write. So much is changing so quickly in the worlds of HR, business, and society overall that attempting to draft a "snapshot" of the challenges facing HR managers almost seemed like an impossible task. Should I focus more on the traditional HR disciplines of recruitment, employee relations, training, compensation, benefits, and the like? Or should I emphasize the changing nature of HR with its emphasis on talent management, data analytics, labor scarcity, remote work, artificial intelligence, and the Fourth Industrial Revolution? I opted to incorporate both approaches into this book as best I could, full well knowing that our profession is on the brink of exploding in terms of its impact on corporate America. In the future, talent, more than capital, will represent *the* critical factor of production. That one statement, reflected in the World Economic Forum's 2020 *Future of Work Report*, tells the whole story about HR's potential.

Speaking of which, the Fourth Industrial Revolution gives us an excellent bridge from this book and its current assumptions about people practices, human capital, organizational agility, and emotional intelligence to take us into the future. Let's start with what the Fourth Industrial Revolution is so that we can gain a broader and more strategic perspective of all that affects our world (including our industry, company, and department) and our roles as HR managers and true partners to our organizations.

THE FIRST INDUSTRIAL REVOLUTION (IR1)
Year: 1784

Hallmarks: steam, coal, and mechanical production equipment

The original industrial revolution transformed the global economy from agriculture to industry. It used water and steam power to *mechanize production*. Coal extraction and the development of the steam engine as well as metal forging completely changed the way goods and products were created and exchanged in a world where "manufacturing" became a prominent driver of economic growth. New tools like the cotton gin (or "cotton engine") totally disrupted and eliminated large swaths of weavers, for example, whose work until that time was done by hand. Canal transportation replaced covered wagons and mule teams and created the first models for today's global supply chain distribution.

THE SECOND INDUSTRIAL REVOLUTION (IR2)
Year: 1870

Hallmarks: Division of labor, mass production, and electricity

If the first industrial revolution was driven by coal, the second revolved around the discovery of electricity, gas, and oil, culminating in the invention of the combustion engine. Both steel-based and chemically based products made their entry onto the world scene, and developments in communication technology produced the telegraph and later the telephone. Transportation grew by leaps and bounds with the invention of the airplane and automobile. Mechanical production grew exponentially through the advent of *mass production*.

THE THIRD INDUSTRIAL REVOLUTION (IR3)

Year: 1969

Hallmarks: IT, electronics, automated production, and the digital revolution

The third industrial revolution focused on the move from mechanical and analog electronic technology to digital electronics. This third wave of revolution used electronics and information technology to *automate production*. Semiconductors, mainframe computing, microprocessors, renewable energy, personal computing, and the World Wide Web roared onto the scene, vastly increasing the potential and global reach of automated production.

THE FOURTH INDUSTRIAL REVOLUTION (IR4)

Year: 2016

Hallmarks: Nano, bio, and IT technologies, 3D printing, artificial intelligence, robotics, quantum computing, and cyber-physical systems

Today, the Fourth Industrial Revolution is being built on its predecessors. The term *Fourth Industrial Revolution* was coined in 2016 by Klaus Schwab, the founder of the World Economic Forum, in a book of the same name. The advanced digital revolution is characterized by a fusion of technologies that is blurring the lines between the physical, digital, and biological spheres. The acceleration of innovation and the velocity of disruption are hard to comprehend or anticipate, but this is where we find ourselves today and why this historical perspective is so important.

Talent development, more so than talent acquisition, will force employers to "grow their own" rather than constantly look externally for new talent. According to the World Economic Forum's 2023 *Future of Jobs Report*, technology is one of the main reasons why incomes have stagnated, or even decreased, for a majority of the population in high-income nations: the demand for highly skilled workers has increased while the demand for workers with less education and lower skills has decreased. The result is a job market with a strong demand at the high and low ends but a hollowing out of the middle. How will this affect any organization's recruitment and development strategies as well as the overall employee experience?

It is against this backdrop that human resources managers and practitioners will need to reinvent themselves and adapt their future leadership practices. Advanced technology, combined with international competition, will require new forms of collaboration, particularly given the speed at which innovation and disruption are taking place (including remote work). And the emergence of global platforms and other new business models means that talent, culture, and organizational structures will have to be rethought and reinvented.

The agile company that incorporates change-management initiatives well will thrive. Overall, the inexorable shift from simple digitization (the Third Industrial Revolution) to innovation based on combinations of technologies (the Fourth Industrial Revolution) will force companies to reexamine the way they do business, particularly in terms of how they will deploy their human resources, retool and upskill their workforce based on new technologies, and compete for talent. The bottom line, however, is that business leaders and HR executives will need to understand their changing environment, challenge the assumptions of their operating teams, and relentlessly and continuously innovate.

This isn't meant to be scary, but it should take your breath away just a little bit. People are truly being recognized as a company's "greatest asset" for the first time: the primary profit lever, the organizational advantage that differentiates top-tier companies from the rest. Human resources will remain the shepherd of that "asset" moving forward. This Fourth Industrial Revolution will change not only what we do but also who we are. It will affect our identity and all the issues associated with it: our sense of privacy, our notions of employment, the time we devote to work and leisure, and how we develop our careers, cultivate our skills, and collaborate with one another.

What will come of compassion, communication, and commitment in this new cyber world? What do "talent," "culture," and "organizational design" really mean relative to the historic responsibilities associated with the human resources function? What new and unforeseen challenges will come our way as a result of generative artificial intelligence? And how does HR measure the contributions of employees and influence talent acquisition, development, and retention in light of these tectonic shifts coming our way? Indeed, technology is affecting all aspects of our working lives and reshaping our economic, social, cultural, and working environments. There has never been a time of greater promise for the HR discipline, although we need to be flexible and agile as it morphs to meet the business world's newest and ever-changing needs.

The effective human resources manager will bend the traditional roles and responsibilities associated with the HR discipline to meet tomorrow's new realities. This shift will require a strong foundation in the basics along with a rejection of traditional, linear thinking and an adoption of a strategic approach to organizational agility and change. I hope *The First-Time Manager: HR* brought you clarity in terms of today's responsibilities and has likewise prepared you for the scope and breadth of tomorrow's challenges. To think strategically about the forces of disruption and innovation shaping our future is an awesome opportunity to create your HR leadership brand. Embrace the change coming your way. *Be* that change. Lead so others will follow you. And make of your life a gift—an opportunity to touch and influence others so they can achieve their own goals, become their best selves, and pay it forward in turn to others who follow in their footsteps.

ACKNOWLEDGMENTS

It takes a whole lot of teamwork and collaboration to prepare a manuscript for publication that covers such a wide breadth of topics. HR is a multifaceted discipline within corporate America that's experiencing tremendous change and growth. Whether we're addressing artificial intelligence, DEI and talent scarcity, remote work, leave of absence management, immigration, public sector and international HR, or the traditional pillars of compensation, benefits, talent acquisition, learning and development, and employee and labor relations, the subject matter experts below were kind enough to share their insights and experiences in reviewing select portions of this manuscript as it made its way through the various rounds of editing. I'm so fortunate to call you all my dearest friends and respected colleagues . . .

Phil Blair, executive officer at Manpower in San Diego.

Christine Bryant, (retired) president and CEO of the San Diego Employers Association.

Barry Coleman, chief operating officer of RealEyes Attention Measurement in Los Angeles.

Larry Comp, CEO and chief innovation officer at LTC Performance Strategies in Valencia, CA.

Debi Conocenti, human resources / wellness and DEI manager at the Motion Picture and Television Fund in Woodland Hills, CA.

Christopher DeFoe, independent HR transformation and technology consultant at DeFoe Associates, LLC, in Jersey City, NJ.

Nina Fleiss, vice president of human resources at The Simons Foundation in New York City.

Andy Forbis, SHRM-SCP, SPHR, principal at Forbis Strategic HR Consulting, LLC, in Raleigh-Durham, NC.

Louis Gutierrez, (former) chief human resources and equity officer at Los Angeles World Airports and CHRO of Paramount Pictures in Hollywood, CA.

Ken Lloyd, PhD, a nationally recognized Southern California HR executive, management consultant, author, and business writer.

Barry Kramer, senior vice president at Chivaroli and Associates Insurance Services in Westlake Village, CA.

Kathie Nirschl, vice president of human resources at Aquarium of the Pacific in Long Beach, CA, recognized by *Forbes* in 2023 as one of the 300 Best Small Employers in the US.

Rachel Spector Whiffin, head of people and culture at SleepScore Labs in Carlsbad, CA.

Bill Stephens, director of client services and the consulting team at Employers Group / Everything HR in El Segundo, CA.

And to the finest legal minds in the labor, employment, and immigration law space . . .

Jacqueline Cookerly Aguilera, partner, labor and employment, at Morgan, Lewis & Bockius LLP in Los Angeles.

Henry Farber, mediator and arbitrator at RanierADR, PLLC in Issaquah, WA.

Alan R. Klein, managing partner and Attorney at Law at Klein & Puri Immigration Law Group, ALC, in Encino, CA.

Jeff Nowak, shareholder at Littler Mendelson in Chicago.

Chris Olmsted, managing shareholder at Ogletree Deakins in La Jolla, CA.

Adam Rosenthal, employment law partner at Sheppard Mullin Richter & Hampton LLP in Del Mar, CA.

APPENDIX 1
The ADA Interactive Tool Kit

**INTERACTIVE PROCESS ACCOMMODATIONS WORKSHEET
FOR EMPLOYEES REPORTING DISABLING CONDITIONS**

Employee Name: _____

Title: _____

Department: _____

I. CURRENT RESTRICTIONS

Include below a description of all of the employee's current reported restrictions (for example, walking, lifting, carrying, climbing, or other activities or actions that the employee must avoid): _____

_____

_____

If restricted from work entirely, date employee stopped work:

_____

"The restrictions listed above match my own understanding of my current restrictions."

X_____   X_____

     Employee Signature   Date

II. DOCUMENTATION

Note: an employer should not ask about the underlying medical cause of an employee's disability and such disclosure is never required.

- ❏ Employee has supporting documentation from health-care provider (name) _____

  - ❏ Provider placed restrictions (noted above) on employee until (date) _____
  - ❏ Provider directed employee to stop work completely until (date) _____
  - ❏ Employee will be able to return to work on the above date (Y/N) _____
  - ❏ Provider's level of confidence in return date (percentage or stated opinion) _____

- ❏ Information from provider needs clarification because

  _____

  _____

- ❏ Clarification has been requested by (date) _____
- ❏ Information from provider is insufficient because:

  - ❏ Provider's explanation of employee's need for accommodation did not include a description of the employee's relevant functional limitations.
  - ❏ Provider does not appear to have expertise to opine on limitations or confirm need for the reasonable accommodation.
  - ❏ Information appears non-credible.

- ❏ Supplemental information has been requested by (date) _____

  _____

Notes:_____

_____

_____

"I understand the above and recognize that my employer need only provide reasonable accommodation when such accommodation is supported by medical documentation."

X_____ X_____
    Employee Signature   Date

III. ACCOMMODATION(S) REQUESTED

Please list, in detail, all accommodations requested by employee:

_____

_____

_____

X_____ X_____
    Employee's Initials   Date

IV. ACCOMMODATION(S) CONSIDERED

Fill out an accommodation box below for each accommodation considered. If leave or reassignment are considered, see V and VI. See Additional Accommodations Form for more space.

Accommodation considered:_____

Date of discussion: _____

Details of accommodation: _____

Accommodation:
- ❏ Offered by employer and accepted by employee.
- ❏ Considered by employer but rejected because employee unable to safely perform essential job functions or employee did not possess occupational qualifications (details) _____

_____

_____

❑ Suggested by employee but rejected by employer because:

_____

_____

_____

❑ Offered by employer but rejected by employee because:

_____

_____

_____

Other considerations and summary of discussion:

_____

_____

_____

"Employee recognizes that refusal to accept an accommodation may render employee unable to perform the essential functions of his or her current position. Employee further recognizes that he or she must participate in the interactive process in good faith and, if possible, communicate directly with the employer."

X_____   X_____

    Employee Signature   Date

Make copies of this Accommodation Request Worksheet (Section III) for additional requests discussed between the employer and the employee.

V. SPECIAL ACCOMMODATION A: REASSIGNMENT TO VACANT POSITION

❑ Employee has provided employer with information on his or her occupational qualifications.

❑ Employee has been given a list of all vacant positions in the company and a preliminary list of positions employer

believes may meet employee's occupational qualifications
and any restrictions.

X_____   X_____
   Employee's Initials   Date

Details of reassignment considered:

_____
_____
_____

Reassignment:
- ❏ Offered by employer and accepted by employee.
- ❏ Considered by employer but rejected because employee
  unable to safely perform essential job functions or
  employee did not possess occupational qualifications.

  (details) _____
  _____
  _____

- ❏ Suggested by employee but rejected by employer because:
  _____
  _____
  _____

- ❏ Offered by employer but rejected by employee because:
  _____
  _____
  _____

- ❏ No open and available position exists for employee's
  restrictions and skill set.

Other considerations and summary of discussion: _____
_____
_____
_____

"Employee recognizes that refusal to accept an accommodation may render employee unable to perform the essential functions of his or her current position. Employee further recognizes that he or she must participate in the interactive process in good faith and, if possible, communicate directly with the employer."

X _____ X _____
       Employee Signature   Date

Make copies of this Accommodation Request Worksheet for additional requests discussed between the employer and the employee.

VI. SPECIAL ACCOMMODATION B: GRANT OR EXTENSION OF LEAVE DUE TO MEDICAL CONDITIONS

Length of leave requested: _____

Date of discussion: _____

Details of leave: _____

_____

_____

_____

Leave:
- ❏ Accepted by employee and given by employer.
- ❏ Suggested by employee but rejected by employer because:

_____

_____

_____

- ❏ Offered by employer but rejected by employee because:

_____

_____

_____

How certain is employee that he or she will return on the leave return date (percentage): _____

Other considerations and summary of discussion: _____

_____

_____

_____

"I understand that I am representing that I currently believe that I will be able to complete the essential job functions of my regularly assigned position upon my return from leave."

X _____   X _____
      Employee Signature   Date

VII. ADDITIONAL EMPLOYEE COMMENTS, QUESTIONS, OR CONCERNS

_____

_____

_____

_____

_____

_____

X _____   X _____
      Employee Signature   Date

X _____   X _____
HR Representative's Signature   Date

APPENDIX 2

Career Advice for a Successful HR Management Career Path

I've enjoyed a successful career across the entertainment, health-care / biotech, and financial service industries, including in nonprofit, international, and union environments. To be sure, it hasn't been all smooth sailing, but I couldn't imagine myself doing anything other than HR because of the opportunities it's given me to touch other people's lives. There's a bit of a ministry in this particular corporate discipline of ours, and I'm happy to share some of the tactics and strategies that I've learned along the way. Consider them but find your own voice and path, remembering that people don't care what you know until they know that you care. Career guidance from the CHRO suite can help, and I'm happy to share mine with you. Use the suggestions that follow to create your own value statements about what you believe, who you choose to be, and how you want to grow your career.

As a general rule, expect the unexpected, explore the unknown, and embrace uncertainty. Learn how to unlearn, get comfortable with ambiguity, and consider the unconventional. This type of agile mindset will serve you well, leading to what scholars refer to as "leadership elasticity," or the ability to transition your leadership style fluidly to be effective in a variety of situations.

1. Always come from an achievement mindset. Don't get lost in the "commas" of managing recruitment, employee relations, compensation, benefits, training, HRIS, and all those other subdisciplines that are sure to keep you busy.

Cut through the fog and focus on quantifying your achievements in terms of dollars and percentages, both for your résumé and LinkedIn profile as well as for your annual self-assessment.

2. Always ask your boss, "How else can I help?" Check in before you go home at night and ask if there's anything else you could do to lend a hand before you leave. Be "that person" who has your boss's back—to the extent possible—to make his or her job easier, to develop a stronger relationship and bond, and to hopefully get exposed to areas beyond your normal job scope because of the strength of your relationship with your immediate superior.

3. Make others better at their jobs. Help people become their best selves. Make it safe for people to seek out your guidance and support. In other words, make of your life a gift. There's no better way for you to excel than to help others excel. The universe is a giant copying machine: what emanates from you returns to you. Be the gift that keeps on giving.

4. Publicly recognize achievements: praise generously in public, censure in private, and assume responsibility for things gone wrong on your team—even if you're not personally responsible. It's your team. All for one and one for all. Model the behaviors you want others to follow. When your people recognize your character and caring, when they realize you have their backs, they'll become loyal to you for the rest of their careers. (And remember that bosses tend to rehire their top performers no matter where they go. That works to your benefit both as a manager and as an employee.)

5. Demonstrate a healthy sense of curiosity. Look to assume responsibilities beyond your immediate area. Endeavor to understand your company's business model and your manager-clients' stressors and challenges. Listen with your

eyes and heart in addition to your ears. Become a trusted resource and coach to your clients and look for opportunities to have their backs and support them, especially through their toughest times. They'll always remember you for that, even years after you've worked together.

6. When it comes to dealing with employees, maintain an open door. Ask people to stop by and visit when they're in the area. Practice management by walking around (MBWA), and check in with employees to see how they're doing, if they need anything, or if there's anything you could do to help. You'll be amazed how much employees appreciate HR managers who make themselves readily available and take the time to ask such a simple question: "How can I help?" Your reputation for trust, respect, and empathy will skyrocket.

7. Teach what you choose to learn. You don't have to be a master to teach mastery. You don't have to wait until you're a CHRO to teach meaningful leadership concepts. The universe knows that you cannot give away something that you don't already have. Therefore, give generously of your time and help others become stronger leaders in their own right. Praise and recognize others, and most important, always come from gratitude and appreciation. Gratitude filters all your experiences—no matter how negative—as an opportunity to thank, trust, and appreciate. When you experience life in gratitude's light, you'll always have a healthy perspective and feel in control.

8. Get certified. SHRM and HRCI offer certification in the HR discipline. You can likewise pursue certification in compensation, benefits, learning and development, and other areas. But having certification credentials next to your name and at the top of your résumé demonstrates your commitment to your chosen field, exposes you to a broad range of topics that might not otherwise come your

way, and helps you stand out among your peers. Be sure to take a prep class, however. In my experience, exams can be tricky in terms of their wording, so it's a good investment to get to know how the tests are structured and questions worded before sitting down for the exam.

9. MBA or professional designation in HR management? That's always a big question for early-career professionals. It depends on what you want to do. While both programs can take two years to complete, there's obviously a world of difference. My best advice: a master's degree will always carry significantly more weight than a professional designation of any sort. Likewise, the costs and time commitment vary tremendously as well. If you pursue an MBA, it's to help you get ahead in the business world in general. If you take a two-year, eight-course professional designation program in human resources management, in comparison, you'll gain deep-dive insights into the various aspects of the HR discipline. I pursued my professional designation in human resource management at UCLA Extension and went on to teach for two decades (and counting). I gained a tremendous network of students and teachers that helped me significantly throughout my HR career. Ultimately, it's up to you: the MBA has much greater career value but won't teach you much about HR, generally speaking. Research which route makes the most sense for you in light of your longer-term career ambitions.

10. Remember the adage "what you want for yourself, give to another." Leadership is the greatest gift the workplace offers because it allows you to touch so many others' lives and careers. When in doubt, err on the side of compassion. Give respect to earn respect. Be there when people feel vulnerable or afraid, especially when it comes to terminations and layoffs. And let people know that you care about them personally and remain available to help them—even after they leave the company. You'll make

lifelong friends and become the HR professional that "everyone seems to remember" for all the right reasons.

Heartfelt leadership will separate you from your peers and help you build strong relationships, networks, and alliances over the coming decades. That's why you're doing all this—to make the (business) world a better place. I hope this book provides some valuable insights and perspective that you can rely on and refer to for years to come. Thanks for permitting me to take this special journey with you!

INDEX

ABOUT THE AUTHOR

PAUL FALCONE (WWW.PAULFALCONEHR.COM) is principal of Paul Falcone Workplace Leadership Consulting, LLC, specializing in management and leadership training, executive coaching, international keynote speaking, and corporate offsite retreats. He's the former chief human resources officer (CHRO) of Nickelodeon Animation Studios and former head of international human resources for Paramount Pictures in Hollywood. Paul served as head of HR for the TV production unit of NBCUniversal, where he oversaw HR operations for NBC's late night and primetime programming lineup, including *The Tonight Show, Saturday Night Live,* and *The Office.* Paul is a renowned expert on effective interviewing and hiring, performance management, and leadership development, especially in terms of helping companies build higher-performing leadership teams. He also has extensive experience in healthcare/ biotech and financial services across international, nonprofit, and union environments.

Paul is the author of a number of HarperCollins Leadership, AMACOM, and SHRM books, many of which have been ranked on Amazon as #1 bestsellers in the areas of human resources management, labor and employment law, business mentoring and coaching, communication in management, and business decision-making and problem-solving. Best-selling books like *101 Tough Conversations to Have with Employees, 101 Sample Write-Ups for Documenting Employee Performance Problems,* and *96 Great Interview Questions to Ask Before You Hire* have been translated into Chinese, Vietnamese, Korean, Indonesian, and Turkish.

Paul is a certified executive coach through the Marshall Goldsmith Stakeholder Centered Coaching program, a long-term contributor to SHRM.org and *HR Magazine*, and an adjunct faculty member in UCLA Extension's School of Business and Management, where he's taught courses on workplace ethics, recruitment and selection, legal aspects of human resources management, and international human resources. He is an accomplished keynote presenter, in-house trainer, and webinar facilitator in the areas of talent management and effective leadership communication.